Painter of the Stars

The Life and Work of
Milton J. Hill
(1887-1972)

Liewer Jordain,

*Ich hoff des glee Buch gebt
dir ebbes gudes un scheenes
aazugucke un aa zu freede.*

Machs Gut mei Freind,

+++

Painter of the Stars

The Life and Work of
Milton J. Hill
(1887-1972)

Lee S. Heffner & Patrick J. Donmoyer

Foreword by Ivan E. Hoyt

Pennsylvania German Cultural Heritage Center
Kutztown University of Pennsylvania

2019

Painter of the Stars: The Life and Work of Milton J. Hill (1887-1972)

By Lee S. Heffner & Patrick J. Donmoyer

Volume VIII of the Annual Publication Series
Pennsylvania German Cultural Heritage Center
Kutztown University of Pennsylvania

Printed in the United States on acid-free paper by Masthof Press, Morgantown, PA

Foreword by Ivan E. Hoyt
Introductory biography by Lee S. Heffner
Preface, chapter texts, and layout by Patrick J. Donmoyer
Cover and frontis photograph courtesy of Beth A. (Hill) Humma of Shire Valley Legacies. www.shirevalleylegacies.com

Photography by the Pennsylvania German Cultural Heritage Center, Kutztown University unless otherwise stated.

Family photographs and ephemera used with permission from Lee S. Heffner, Beth A. (Hill) Humma of Shire Valley Legacies, Dorian (Derr) Fetherolf, the Family of Harold J. & Esther L. (Hill) Derr, and other members of the Hill Family.

Compilation Copyright © 2020

Pennsylvania German Cultural Heritage Center, Kutztown University

All rights reserved. No part of this book may be reprinted or reproduced or utilized in any form or by any electronic, mechanical or other means, now known or hereafter invented, including photocopying and recording or in any information storage or retrieval system, without permission in writing from the author and the publisher.

ISBN: 978-0-9987074-5-7
Library of Congress Control Number: 2020920309

22 Luckenbill Road
Kutztown, Pennsylvania
19530
(610) 683-1589
heritage@kutztown.edu
www.kutztown.edu/pgchc

Masthof Press
219 Mill Road
Morgantown, PA
19543
(610) 286-0258
www.masthof.com

In Memory

of

Milton J. & Gertrude D. (Strausser) Hill.

Dedicated to all of

the extended Hill Family

and *Freindschaft*.

Contents

PREFACE:
By Patrick J. Donmoyer   9

FOREWORD:
A Tribute to Milton Hill by Ivan E. Hoyt   13

INTRODUCTION:
A Grandson's Memories by Lee S. Heffner   15

CHAPTER I. The Hill Family   21

CHAPTER II. Painter of the Stars   29

CHAPTER III. Gertrude D. Hill & the Family Farm   43

CHAPTER IV. Magical Misconceptions   61

CHAPTER V. A Tradition Evolves   69

CHAPTER VI. An Artist's Epilogue   91

CHAPTER VII. An Open-Air Gallery   95
Historic & Contemporary Decorated Barns

CHAPTER VIII. Inspired Artistry   121
Contemporary Art in the Spirit of Milton J. Hill

ENDNOTES   133
BIBLIOGRAPHY   139
INDEX   141

Acknowledgments

Sincere heartfelt thanks to my dear mother, the late Ellen E. (Hill) Heffner, for saving an incredible collection of artifacts of her father, Milton Jacob Hill. She was a constant inspiration and support throughout my life, instilling in me a deep appreciation for family heritage and ancestry.

My grandparents, Milton J. and Gertrude D. (Strausser) Hill were also incredibly supportive and influential in my life, especially gifting me with the farm work ethic and sharing with me their love of the Pennsylvania German (Dutch) language. I visualize smiles of approval on their faces looking down from their heavenly home at the publication of this volume.

Special appreciation to Ivan E. Hoyt, Master Artisan, Pennsylvania Guild of Craftsmen, for his inspirational foreword, commemorating my grandfather, Milton J. Hill.

I owe my deepest thanks and recognition to Patrick J. Donmoyer, director of the Pennsylvania German Cultural Heritage Center (PGCHC) at Kutztown University, for his guidance and wisdom in the world of publishing. This commemorative work, *Painter of the Stars: The Life and Work of Milton J. Hill (1887-1972)*, would not have been possible without his expertise, support, and collaboration.

To everyone involved in this milestone accomplishment, friendships that last a lifetime are an amazing blessing. All honor and blessing are yours, our Heavenly Father and Creator!

Respectfully,

Lee S. Heffner

I would like to express my gratitude for the opportunity to contribute to this folk-cultural homage to the life and work of Milton J. Hill. Although I never had the honor to know him in person, I am deeply grateful to have witnessed his enduring spirit in members of his extended family and throughout the whole Hill *Freindschaft*.

For the many contributions of Esther L. (Hill) Derr, daughter of Milton Hill, and her husband Harold J. Derr for their willingness to share their memories of Milton and the Hill family history during the preliminary research for this work. The Pennsylvania German Cultural Heritage Center at Kutztown University is honored by the generous donations from Esther and Harold of culturally significant artifacts that tell the story of Milton Hill and his artwork.

With gratitude to Dorian (Derr) Fetherolf for her welcoming support of this project in sharing so many significant memories, photographs, footage, and pieces of family history with us.

A special thanks to Bart Hill, great grandson of Milton J. Hill, for the generous donation of four original Milton Hill barn stars from Windsor Castle.

With sincere appreciation to Beth A. (Hill) Humma of Shire Valley Legacies, for her superb genealogical work and willingness to let us use selected Hill family photographs in this project.

I am especially grateful for Lee S. Heffner, whose collaborative spirit, clear memory, and meticulous attention to detail have made this work not only possible but a pleasure to co-create. Lee's awareness of the nuances of his grandfather's life and the care with which he has preserved the history of his family is graciously matched by a heartfelt desire to share this story with the community. I am honored by his friendship, thoughtful guidance, and dedication.

Mit hatzliche Dank,

Patrick J. Donmoyer

Preface

Milton Hill: Painter of the Stars

Patrick J. Donmoyer

On behalf of the Pennsylvania German Cultural Heritage Center at Kutztown University, we are honored to present this celebration of the life and work of the preeminent barn star painter Milton J. Hill (1887-1972) of Virginville, Berks County. Milton's artistic career roughly spanned the first three quarters of the twentieth century, a time of momentous change for his Pennsylvania Dutch community and for American society as a whole. Milton's art embraced this era of transition, demonstrating vast the potential for regional folk art to embody and sustain the complex cultural identities of ethnic communities, through a rootedness in tradition and an openness to new forms of folk-cultural expression.

As a barn star painter, Milton created circular geometric murals of colorful star patterns in series on the facades of Pennsylvania barns, an artistic practice which developed over many generations throughout the region. These murals first appeared on vernacular architecture in the regional landscape in the decades following the American Revolution and became firmly established as a classic form of traditional folk art by the middle of the 19th century. At the age of 14, Milton learned his methods and techniques from his father who was also a painter, who had learned from his father before him, making Milton a third generation painter in the barn star tradition.

Milton Hill was both a folk artist and an innovator. His crowning achievement was the development of a unique signature barn star pattern, which remains one of the most visually complex and desirable of its kind throughout the region, even after well over a century since he first created it around 1910. Although by definition, folk art favors traditional forms, maintaining a sense of continuity over many generations, Milton was able to successfully introduce new patterns that did not so much seek to challenge the parameters of his field, but rather expanded them to include a broader range of artistic possibilities in the first few decades of the twentieth century.

Later in his career, by pioneering new techniques, designs, and formats, including painting on commercial signboard, Milton built upon his traditional background to launch the next evolution of the art form in

Above: A Milton Hill star, repainted by Johnny Claypoole (1921-2004) of Lenhartsville, Berks County.
Opposite: The Rausch Barn in Perry Township, originally painted by Milton Hill, and later repainted by Donald I. Smith in the late 1990s. *Survey of Decorated Barns, Patrick J. Donmoyer 2007-2020.*

the 1950s. This coincided with the creation of large nationally recognized folklife celebrations, such as the Kutztown Folk Festival, which introduced his work to broader American audiences of visitors and tourists interested in the region's culture.

As a speaker of Pennsylvania Dutch, Milton represented his community's unique cultural experience during a time of both increased attention from visitors, but also rampant misrepresentation. Milton produced his work with integrity, and refused to cater to the growing body of popular misconceptions that sought to capitalize on the false conflation of the barn star tradition with the supernatural. The misnomer of the fabled 'hex sign' with its promise of mystery and magic was in fact a notion that developed long after the Hill family had already been painting throughout the region for generations.

Milton witnessed the development of this tourist narrative created by travel writers when he was already decades into his own career, and offered the authentic alternative consistent with the folk-culture in which he was born and raised. His work was an artistic celebration of color and celestial geometry, created for the pure pleasure of visual appreciation. It is against this bifurcated backdrop of community identity and national sensation that the 'hex sign,' for better or worse, became the controversial symbol of Pennsylvania Dutch ethnicity and culture in the United States, while the original term 'barn star' remains prominent only in a handful of counties in Southeastern Pennsylvania where the tradition originally began. In light of this controversy, the work of Milton Hill becomes all the more important in rediscovering the origins and interpretation of this unique form of regional American folk art.

Milton Hill is therefore not only worthy of celebration for his ability to authentically represent his local cultural traditions to national audiences, but especially for his willingness to shape the tradition in new ways, which has inspired new generations of artists well into the present day.

My own personal connection to Milton Hill began in 2007, while conducting preliminary research for a systematic survey of all of the decorated barns in Berks County—the epicenter of this folk-cultural artistic expression. My survey of the barns was motivated by a desire to document and preserve the tradition, due to the general consensus that the art form was fading into obscurity with the loss of many historic barns through neglect or development. At the time, there were estimated to be only a few hundred decorated barns left in the entire region of Southeastern Pennsylvania. However, the results of the survey were surprising.

During the summer of 2008, I documented over 450 decorated barns concentrated especially in northern Berks County just south of the Blue Mountain, and later scores more throughout Lehigh, Montgomery, Bucks, Schuylkill and Northampton. The results confirmed that not only were there far more decorated barns than previously imagined, but furthermore, evidence suggested that the number of barns decorated each year far outnumbered the loss of decorated barns, confirming that the art of barn star painting is a vibrant living tradition and viable expression of folk-cultural identity continuing in the present day.

Just over a dozen of these examples, concentrated in the area around Virginville, were all that remained of Milton Hill's prolific career and artistic presence in the landscape. Nevertheless, these few examples stood out as focal points in the rural community and as some of the most highly sophisticated examples of the tradition anywhere in Pennsylvania. In 2010, I interviewed Milton Hill's daughter Esther and her husband Harold Derr, as well as Milton Hill's grandson Lee Heffner. This interview formed the foundation of "Milton Hill: The Star Painter" a chapter included in my folk-cultural study of the tradition *Hex Signs: Myth and Meaning in Pennsylvania Dutch Barn Stars,* released in 2013. Milton Hill also later became the focal point of a collaborative exhibition with Glencairn Museum, entitled *Hex Signs: Sacred and Celestial Symbolism in Pennsylvania Dutch Barn Stars* in 2019.

Shortly after my initial interview with members of the Hill family, Lee Heffner expressed his interest in creating a book to honor his grandfather's work in more depth. Although I initially encouraged Lee's plans to pursue the book solo and offered to make available many of the resources I had collected, Lee later approached me in 2018 with the desire to collaborate on the Milton Hill biography. Lee compiled a concise biographical introduction, copious notes and reflections, and organized a wide range of original family ephemera. While I supplied the majority of the written narrative, I depended heavily upon Lee's precision and intimate knowledge of the Hill family to produce the content. In certain portions of the study, I took the lead in researching the specific barns that Milton painted, his family history, as well as his role at the Kutztown Folk Festival, and any errors and omissions are entirely my own.

This new collaborative folk-cultural study of Milton Hill begins with a tribute by seasoned hex sign artist Ivan Hoyt, and a concise biography of Milton Hill by Lee Heffner, entitled "A Grandson's Memories." The chapters begin with Milton's family and community context, connecting Milton's experiences and sense of place on the Hill farm with the story of his ancestors' transatlantic immigration and settlement in Berks County in the early eighteenth century. Next, Milton's connection to the tradition and work of barn star painting is explored in the second chapter, highlighting his techniques, materials, processes, and projects. The third chapter explores the Hill family farm as a venue for living tradition, fostered by the efforts of his wife, Gertrude D. (Strausser) Hill as the primary farmer and facilitator of Milton's artistic career. We explore the conflicting narratives surrounding twentieth-century tourist literature and the rise of the "hex sign" in pop culture in the fourth chapter. In the following chapter we showcase the evolution of Milton's work and his influence on the tradition as a whole through the Kutztown Folk Festival and its national appeal. An epilogue describes Milton's retirement and final years with his family, and the following two gallery chapters showcase his work on local barns past and present, and the persistence of Milton's classic designs among new generations of painters.

We hope that this celebration of Milton Hill's life and work will serve to further the exploration of unique American cultural communities throughout the United States, and will be a welcome and cherished tribute in Milton Hill's home community in the rolling hills of Berks County. It is also my desire that this work will introduce Milton Hill to new audiences and inspire future generations of artists to become bearers of tradition in their communities, and, from Milton's legacy, to learn the value of innovation, change, and adaptation in sustaining a region's vibrant folk culture.

Patrick J. Donmoyer
October 6, 2020
German-American Day

Above: A Milton Hill star in Perry Township, repainted by barn star artist Eric Claypoole of Lenhartsville, Berks County. *Survey of Decorated Barns, Patrick J. Donmoyer 2007-2020.*

FOREWORD

A Tribute to Milton Hill

Ivan E. Hoyt

For the last forty-seven years of my life, I have been deeply intrigued by the Pennsylvania Dutch folk tradition of decorating their barns with barn stars, commonly known today as hex signs. I have designed and hand painted hex signs, studied their history, written about them, and taught the folk art to children and adults. Although I have been educated in the visual arts and fine art, I consider myself "self-taught" in the folk art of hex signs. None of my formal education prepared me for the tools or techniques I needed to make hex signs.

My folk art education, like all folk artists, was provided by observation and study of those who went before as I tried to follow my own direction. In particular, I was deeply influenced in this folk art by the subject of this volume, the late Milton J. Hill of Virginville, Berks County, Pennsylvania. I believe my credentials and longevity working in the folk art of hex sign painting gives me a unique perspective to offer on this truly talented Pennsylvanian and American treasure.

To illustrate the reverence held in my family for Milton Hill, let me relate a short anecdote. One Saturday afternoon I was watching my favorite home improvement show, when my son Eli told me my older son, Ethan, was on the telephone. I told Eli to tell him I would call him back after the program. Eli said two words "Milton Hill," and I immediately said, "give me the phone." Ethan was at an antique mall where he found a 13" hand painted Milton Hill hex sign. I asked him how he knew it was a Milton Hill original, because Hill did not usually sign his work. He told me that the sign had a yellowed, aged label on the back that read "Made and Designed by Milton J. Hill, Hamburg, R. D. 2, PA." That alone was evidence of its originality but I asked Ethan to check one more element, whether the sign had scribe marks defining the design shapes. It was Hill's custom to

Above: A monochromatic Milton Hill Star, painted by Ivan E. Hoyt, 2013. *Heilman Collection.*
Left: A detail of an adapted Hill Star pattern painted on weathered barn boards by Ivan E. Hoyt in 2019, and on display at the Kutztown Folk Festival. *Courtesy of Ivan E. Hoyt & Family.*

scribe or etch the design into the surface rather than draw it with a pencil or chalk. When my son confirmed the scribe marks, I was ecstatic and it is now one of the most valued pieces in my Pennsylvania Dutch folk art collection. Old time antique collectors would say finding an original Milton Hill painting is "as rare as hen's teeth." In four decades of collecting, it is the only one I have found.

So often, especially among the Pennsylvania Dutch, we take our culture for granted. Established cultural traditions are right in front of us and we just don't see them or feel they are significant. When Milton Hill was approached by Alfred Shoemaker, one of the founders of the Kutztown Folk Festival in the early 1950s, he was reluctant to put his skills on display. He soon learned that what he did was very special and a unique part of the Pennsylvania Dutch culture that people wanted to share. The popular demand for his work necessitated that he paint on plywood and Masonite surfaces that were more portable than the barn boards he was comfortable painting, thus he made an innovation that facilitates my work and that of my contemporaries.

More important than the surface on which he painted, was the artistic skill that Milton Hill brought to the folk art of barn star painting. Hill followed the early tradition of decorating the forebay section of the bank barns exclusively with geometric stars and rosettes. He referred to the designs as barn stars and never used the term "hex sign" to describe his work.

Limiting his repertoire to stars and rosettes in no way limited his artistic genius. Using common tools including a compass, straight edge, and square, Hill was a master of geometric design. His most well known barn star is based on an eight-pointed design, with the star faceted into smaller and smaller stars that achieved an optical effect of movement. This star is almost always bordered by scallops of blue that appear to overlap as the value (shade) of blue transitions from dark to light. This outstanding design is referred to by all contemporary hex sign painters as the "Hill Star" in homage to its creator. Many of Milton Hill's extraordinary barn stars have such an intricacy and complexity that you almost think you were looking through a kaleidoscope and yet they were the creation of a very humble man. When asked why he painted his beautiful stars, he said "Chust fer Nice" or "Chust fer So."

Lee Heffner will take you back to a time when a young Milton, age 14, apprenticed with his father learning the barn painting trade and also learning the professional skills to make him a master of his trade. As Milton Hill grew to be the leader of his barn painting crew, he controlled the quality of his work from the very beginning. Not counting on the quality of store-bought "patent paint," Hill preferred instead to order his chemicals and pigment in bulk and carefully formulate his own mix. His reputation for quality was of utmost importance. It was also important to show people he conducted his trade as a professional. Milton Hill was proud of his skills, and he dressed to exhibit professionalism. White painter's bib overalls, shirt, painter's cap, gentleman's tie, and white painter's coat let his patrons know he was a professional. In my opinion, Milton J. Hill represented a time in Pennsylvania history when pride and excellence in your work was the rule rather than the exception, and through his dedication to his art, he enriched Pennsylvania Dutch culture.

June 3, 2019
Ivan E. Hoyt
Master Artisan,
Pennsylvania Guild of Craftsmen

INTRODUCTION

A Grandson's Memories of Milton J. Hill

Lee S. Heffner

Milton J. Hill, a prominent craftsman-painter from the Virginville area, was born on March 23, 1887 in the same farmhouse where he passed away on January 2, 1972.

During his 84-year lifespan, Milton and his wife, Gertrude D. (Strausser) Hill earned their living on the family dairy farm. They were the parents of five children (in order of their birth), John L., Jacob W., Ellen E. (Hill) Heffner, Milton D., and Esther L. (Hill) Derr. Their last surviving daughter, Esther, passed away at the age of 91 on June 4, 2019.

During his early career, Milton along with his two oldest sons, John and Jacob, and later his son-in-law Stanley O. Heffner, and his youngest son, Milton, contracted many painting and interior decorating jobs in the area. Milton and his work crew also traveled to the city of Reading, Berks County, Pennsylvania where he and his co-workers renovated and redecorated the homes and offices of several prominent physicians during the 1920s-1940s.

Milton was also very proud of the jobs he secured at Lauer's Brewery. He was a regular customer for many years at Stichter's Hardware Store at 505-509 Penn Street in Reading. Because of the store's expansive and quality inventory, Milton would remark that if Stichter's didn't have what you needed, you couldn't purchase it in Reading.

During Milton's one-room school years, he developed an avid interest in the geometric designs that he reluctantly listened to tourists years later refer to as "hex signs". Milton called his creations barn stars or barn decorations.

Initially, Milton and his work crew inscribed and painted the famous "Hill Stars" directly on the barn walls, standing on ladders and swings for hours at a time to accomplish this precise, tedious work.

Milton's oldest son, John, was also an excellent artist. For many years he painted pictures of horses, cows, and other farm animals with a natural background of clouds, blue sky, trees and soil.

In 1953 at the Kutztown Folk Festival, Milton embarked on his opportunity of a lifetime to be involved as a local craftsman to design, paint, and offer for sale, his many

A Milton Hill star re-creation, painted on weathered barn wood at the Kutztown Folk Festival in 2016, modeled after Milton's classic stars from the Leiby Homestead in Virginville, Berks County, ca. 1940. *Pennsylvania German Cultural Heritage Center, Kutztown University.*

barn stars. In order for prospective buyers to have these barn stars in hand, Milton began using Masonite, which he referred to as tempered pressed wood. Very durable in the weather, Milton used a coping saw to cut the discs from wooden sheets in the farm chicken house.

Milton Hill was extremely pleased with the frequent visits to his farm by one of the founders of the Kutztown Folk Festival, Dr. Alfred L. Shoemaker. In addition to Dr. Shoemaker, two other founders of the festival were Drs. Don Yoder and J. William Frey. They were also editors of *The Pennsylvania Dutchman,* which first began as a weekly newspaper published by the Pennsylvania Dutch Folklore Center, Inc., located at the Fackenthal Library on the campus of Franklin and Marshall College in Lancaster.

Olive G. Zehner, Festival receptionist and program director, also accompanied Dr. Shoemaker to the Hill farm in order to enlist Milton's talents for the sixteen years where he demonstrated his artistic skills and sold his barn stars to many tourists.

Milton was particularly proud of the fact that his artwork is present in many of our country's states, and also abroad, especially in Europe.

It was during my formative years that my grandfather tried his best to engage me in learning his artistic skills. However, I was immersed in farm life activities, assisting his wife, my grandmother, Gertrude, in all those chores of a family farm in the mid 1950's and up until the end of 1964. I lived on the farm with my grandparents for two and a half years from June 1962 to December 1964.

Some of the most treasured and memorable experiences helped me to develop a strong work ethic. Field work included plowing, discing, and harrowing the soil for planting, cultivating corn, cutting and baling hay and straw, bagging grain on the tractor drawn combine, silo filling, cutting wood for my grandfather's wood-coal stove in his paint shop with a mounted saw on the F20 Farmall tractor.

Grandmother and I were in the barn at 4:30 AM every morning milking the dairy cows with electric milking machines (my job) while she had a number of chosen cows that she hand-milked. During these years milk was transported to the dairy in milk cans. Other than unusual circumstances, the milk truck driver arrived rather promptly by 6 a.m. for pickup.

Milton Hill relaxing in his studio at home, brushes in hand. *Courtesy of Lee S. Heffner & Family.*

Opposite: Three original Milton Hill stars, painted on 24" masonite disks in his later artistic style, when he demonstrated at the Kutztown Folk Festival in the 1950s and 60s. Because this later work was on modular disks and painted in the comfort of a studio, it allowed him a degree of freedom and experimentation beyond what he could have achieved only painting on barns. Milton's grandson Lee Heffner purchased the thirty-two-pointed star (top) from Milton for $18 in the 1960s. *Courtesy of Lee S. Heffner & Family.*

My grandmother was my second Mom! I especially treasure our time together while she sat on the iron seat of the five-foot sickle bar McCormick-Deering grass mower, lowering and raising the bar when needed as we mowed acres of alfalfa and timothy grass with the F14 Farmall tractor to be dried for baling with the New Holland 77 baler.

When my grandmother was busy canning summer fruits such as peaches, pears, cherries, etc., or making quince jelly, my Aunt Esther Derr, the Hills' youngest daughter, would occupy the grass mower seat in her place.

In retrospect, I have regretted my lack of more mature foresight in not learning my grandfather's artistic barn star skills. However, since I accepted the role of farmer-in-residence, this allowed Milton to enjoy long periods of time to prepare his barn star inventory for each Kutztown Folk Festival.

During the last five years, his daughter, Esther Derr, assisted her father in painting many barn stars. She had a very steady hand, a trait from her father.

Milton's final festival year was 1968. He was at the time having health issues. Whenever I would visit with my grandparents after Milton's retirement from the festival, he would reminisce about his entire artistic career. Milton would often

Milton Hill with two of his distinctive stars in the Parking Lot of the Kutztown Folk Festival in 1960. Photograph by Lee. S. Heffner, Grandson of Milton J. Hill.

share fond memories of our "trips" to Virginville. I accompanied him, first riding in his 1935 Chevrolet, and later in his 1950 Buick Special.

He shared younger experiences of prominent business people in the Virginville community. Included were the following: Dr. Milton Fritch, family medical doctor (for whom he was named), members of the Dreibelbis family, especially William, who operated the general store, Myers Balthaser Dodge-Plymouth Car Dealership, Harry Dreibelbis, shoemaker, Chester and Esther Homan, who manned the combination post office and general store, and Russell Moyer, farm supply and feed mill owner.

Milton also reminisced about the following craftsmen he had the privilege of enjoying their company at the Kutztown Folk Festival: Ollie Strausser, the harmonica playing basketmaker from Pricetown (a distant relative of Milton's wife, Gertrude), Charles Wagenhurst, tinsmith of Kutztown, Anson Stump of Kempton, wheelwright, and Viola Miller, funnel cake lady of the original Pennsylvania Dutch funnel cake stand.

Another vivid memory of my grandfather is his love for the concerts of the Allentown Band, then under the direction of Dr. Albertus L. Meyers. Milton followed the band frequently at its summer and early fall performances in the region. I became the chauffeur for the last several concerts. My grandfather really enjoyed the first Sunday in August "Kutztown Day" concerts and those at Lobachsville, Pike Township, Berks County.

Many people were not aware of Milton's beautiful flowing handwriting style. I myself have always been meticulous with fine, legible handwriting. Maybe this is an inherited trait via my grandfather and my mother, Ellen, who also had beautifully formed penmanship.

Finally, permit me to introduce myself by sharing a brief history of my educational background. I graduated salutatorian of my 1962 Perry Township High School class located at 4th and Reber Streets in Shoemakersville, Pennsylvania. That summer, I became the farmer-in-residence for the next two and one half years.

Since there was no opportunity for me to acquire the family farm, my education was continued at Kutztown State College (1965-1968) with a B.S. Degree in Elementary Education, followed by an M.Ed. Degree (1974) in the same field. A Principal's Certificate was earned at Lehigh University in Bethlehem in 1981.

My thirty-five year educational career was completed in December 2003. I taught Fourth Grade for twenty-four years, followed by an eleven-year position as Assistant Elementary Principal, all in the Hamburg Area School District.

In closing, over the years, a number of friends and other residents of the Virginville area have remarked that Milton J. Hill never really received the credit due him for his artistic contributions. My sincere appreciation for supporting my grandfather's legacy goes to three special men. They are: Ivan Hoyt, hex sign painter and veteran participant in the annual Kutztown Folk Festival, who has given me constant encouragement to memorialize my grandfather in print; Eric Claypoole, another very talented barn star designer and painter, who continually reveres the Hill Star; and last but not least, Patrick J. Donmoyer, director of the Pennsylvania German Cultural Heritage Center at Kutztown University, who has graciously offered his professional skills to compile my collection of artifacts on Milton J. Hill. Mr. Donmoyer has memorialized my grandfather in "Milton Hill: The Star Painter," Chapter 8, *Hex Signs: Myth & Meaning in Pennsylvania Dutch Barn Stars*, the 2013 annual publication of the Pennsylvania German Cultural Heritage Center, Kutztown University.

Appreciatively,

Lee S. Heffner

Grandson of Milton J. Hill

Above: As Lee S. Heffner recalls: "This barn star was made and designed by my maternal grandfather, Milton J. Hill, barn star decorator, at his kitchen table in the family farmhouse in the mid 1950s. I, Lee S. Heffner, observed granddad draw this barn star with a compass and straight edge. He advised me how to pencil color the decoration."

The German-language birth and baptismal certificate (*Taufschein*) of Milton J. Hill, which reads in translation: "Mr. John M. Hill of Perry Township, Berks County, PA, and his spouse Ellen Elizabeth (nee Wanner) of Perry Township, on the 23rd of March, 1887, in Perry Township, Berks County, PA, a son was born, which received Holy Baptism on the 3rd of July, 1887, and the name Milton Jacob. The witnesses were the parents themselves. This was certified by the Rev. Benjamin Weiss, Reformed minister at Zion Union Church, Perry Township, Berks County."

Pennsylvania German Cultural Heritage Center, Kutztown University. Gift of Harold & Esther (Hill) Derr & Family.

CHAPTER I

The Hill Family

Nestled in the rolling hills just northwest of Virginville, Berks County, a creative and enterprising Pennsylvania Dutch family settled and established a farm near the border of what is today Perry and Windsor townships. After many generations, the Hill family and their descendants number in the thousands, and among them was Milton J. Hill, the most celebrated barn star painter in the history of Pennsylvania.

The Hill family, like many other German-speaking immigrants of the eighteenth century, left behind their ancestral homes to seek new opportunities for a fresh start in Pennsylvania.

Fleeing an over-populated German countryside that was economically devastated by generations of wars over territory and religion, Johann Jacob Hill (1689-1739) and his wife Anna Elisabetha (Müller) Hill (1691-1774) along with their numerous children, left their rural community at Lambsheim, in the vicinity of Frankenthal in the Rhineland-Pfalz.[1] Like thousands of families throughout Southwestern Germany, Switzerland, Alsace, and neighboring regions, they made their way up the Rhine River toward the port cities of the Netherlands along the North Sea, where they departed for the New World.

After roughly two months at sea, weathering storms, sickness, and meager rations, the Hill family arrived at the port of Philadelphia, Pennsylvania where all males over the age of 16 were compelled to take an oath to the British crown.[2]

Although their names appear in none of the well-preserved ship manifests of the era, and virtually nothing remains of their immigration story, early church registers record the family's involvement in Lutheran congregations in Heuchelheim and, possibly, Meisenheim in the Rhineland-Pfalz, Germany, and later in Moselem, Berks County, Pennsylvania. Collectively these records document the family's marriages and baptisms, and offer insights into the approximate time of their arrival in the New World sometime between 1720-1727.[3]

The Hills originally settled at Moselem, Berks County (then part of Philadelphia County) along with another family from Lambsheim, the Merkels, who likely emigrated around the same time. The Hills were among the earliest founding families of Zion Moselem Lutheran Church, which established a congregation in 1737[5] and the Hill patriarch Johann Jacob was one of three individuals to initiate the building of a log meetinghouse church in 1739, although he died later the same year.[6]

While some of the offspring of Johann Jacob and Anna Elizabetha Hill left the area and headed west,[7] most of the sons and daughters settled in rural Berks County where their descendants remain today.

One son, Johann Jacob Hill the younger, (1716-1775), who was born in Lambsheim, Germany prior to the family's immigration, married Maria Apollonia Merkel (1719-1774) in 1739. Maria Apollonia was also from Lambsheim, and had attended the same Lutheran church in nearby Heuchelheim.[8] Together they settled on 200 acres of land in Windsor Township (present-day Perry Township). The original land grant

Dietrich
420 MAIN ST., KUTZTOWN, PA.

records indicate that, after having his land warranted in 1738 and surveyed in 1739, "in consideration of 31 Pounds," John Jacob Hill was granted the land on October 15, 1747.[9] "Jacob Hill Sr.," as he would later appear in local tax records in Windsor Township,[10] was officially naturalized in 1765 as a citizen of Pennsylvania. His 200 acres of land and original homestead eventually was subdivided into two contiguous farms in Perry Township, which sustained the Hill family for generations. In 1887, it was also where Milton J. Hill was born and raised, and, eventually, where he passed away in 1972.

Milton Jacob Hill was born into the world on a cold rainy day on March 23, 1887 to John M. Hill (1855-1933) and Ellen Elizabeth (Wanner) Hill (1857-1936) in an old story-and-a-half stone farm house, and the oldest structure on the Hill farm.

Together, John and Ellen ran a modest farming operation, and John also painted houses and barns as a supplement to their agricultural income. By the time that John was managing the farm, the property had already been divided between his parents, Jacob Hill Jr. (b. 1818) and Mary (Miller) Hill (1822-1880), and his grandparents, Jacob Hill Sr. (1789-1885) and Magdalena (Strausser) Hill (1800-1866).[11] The latter farm was eventually bought by the Schappell family, and the Hills were finally left with the homestead and approximately 80 acres of the original land grant's 200 acre tract.

John was remembered by subsequent generations as a devout Lutheran who read his German Bible every day.[12] The family was part of their ancestral congregation at Zion Union Church in Windsor Castle, where the Hills were among a number of Lutheran congregants historically connected to Zion Moselem Church, who split off in 1759 to form a Union Church with Zion Reformed Church.[13] It was at the Union church where Milton J. Hill was baptized on July 3, 1887.[14] Milton was the middle child of three siblings, with an older sister, Cecilia W. (Hill) Dries (1881-1907), and a younger brother, John Tyburtis Hill (1892-1988).

The Hill family spoke Pennsylvania Dutch in the home, and used English only as a second language.[15] Previous generations used standard German in the churches, but they gradually began to shift toward widespread use of English in local congregations before the beginning of the twentieth century.

Nevertheless, for the Hill family, Pennsylvania Dutch was the primary spoken language in the home and on the farm well into the twentieth century, and it was the first language that Milton Hill learned as a child.

According to family accounts, Milton's very first word as a baby was in Pennsylvania Dutch, and the word was *"neinzich"* (ninety). Although he would only live to be 84, his relatives joked that this word portended that he would one day reach the ripe old age of 90.

Above: Family photograph of Milton J. Hill, ca. 1890. Note that his dress is traditional attire for all toddlers in the nineteenth century, regardless of the gender of the child. *Courtesy of Lee S. Heffner & Family.*

Opposite: Cabinet photograph of John M. Hill (1855-1933), seated with his two sons, (left to right) Milton J. (1887-1972) and John T. (1892-1988). *Courtesy of Lee S. Heffner & Family.*

Milton grew up on the Hill farm, and attended six grades of school at the Virginville one-room schoolhouse, where he learned the meticulous penmanship that stayed with him his whole life. Milton also showed a budding ability in geometry and art, and his teacher, Jeremiah P. Adam (1880-1966),[16] encouraged the development of his skills and interest. Sometime around 1899, when Milton completed his final year of school in the sixth grade, he produced a series of sophisticated watercolor illustrations of geometric barn star patterns on heavy wood-pulp paper.

Although none of these paintings feature the classic pattern that would later be called "The Milton Hill Star" by subsequent generations, these early designs do show elements that appeared in some of Milton's later work in the 1950s and 1960s, such as the overlapping sixteen-pointed star pattern, and the heavy, solid blue, scalloped border.

The paintings are extremely advanced even for a child as precocious as Milton must have been, and the complexity of the stars is matched only by the accuracy of their rendering in full color. What is most evident in these illustrations is that, even at such a young age, Milton had already begun to develop a distinctive style that would continue to set his artistic work apart from that of all others in his time. Later, and throughout his career as a painter, he carried these fragile mementos of his childhood carefully folded and tucked into his toolbox, showing them only to a select few who showed great interest in his work.[17]

Undoubtedly, Milton's father, John must have played a role in nurturing his son's early interest in painting. As a painter himself, John was very likely the artist behind the four intricate stars that appear in early photographs of the Hill family barn from sometime after 1910 (see opposite page). The stars were already showing significant weathering and age at the time that the photograph was taken, suggesting John's hand, rather than Milton's. Furthermore, the barn features seven-pointed stars with alternating colors of yellow and black on each point against a white background, with a solid black border, and are quite unlike Milton's signature work. Although the arrangement is fairly simple, the geometry of dividing a circle by seven, with approximately 51.4 degrees between each star point, requires some serious skill in drafting. This suggests that John may have been equally interested in geometry, like his son Milton.

As Milton grew, he nurtured not only his artistic side, but also his budding horticultural and engineering interests. In his early years out of school, when he was still a farmhand for his father's operation, Milton

Three early watercolor paintings by Milton J. Hill from his childhood days in the one-room schoolhouse ca. 1899. *Pennsylvania German Cultural Heritage Center, Kutztown University. Gift of Harold & Esther (Hill) Derr &Family.*

Above: Date-board for the barn of Jacob Hill Sr. (1789-1885) and Magdalena (Strausser) Hill (1800-1866), located west of the Hill homestead, on land originally belonging to the 200 acre Hill land grant. Pennsylvania German Cultural Heritage Center, Kutztown University. Gift of Harold & Esther (Hill) Derr &Family.

Below: Early photograph of the Hill barn, ca. 1910, featuring John M. Hill, Maurice J. Dries, "Cass" Catherine S. (Berstler) Hill, Gertrude D. Strausser Hill, and John T. Hill. Courtesy of Lee S. Heffner & Family.

began a nursery for fruit trees, bushes, and vines which he purchased, selectively grafted, and sold. He collected a wide variety of apples, pears, peaches, cherries, quince, apricots, plums, grapes, currants, gooseberries, and even nut trees—many of which would be considered heirloom varieties today, for their cultural and regional significance.[18] Milton's inventory itemized rare apple varieties such as Wolf River, a cold-hardy variety with enormous fruit, treasured for producing smooth, high-quality *Lattwarrick* (applebutter), or Winter Banana, a fragrant dessert apple, with the rare ability to self-pollinate, as well as scores of early varieties such as Belle de Boskoop apple, Worden Seckel pear, St. Ambrose apricots, Reas Mammoth quince, Fay's Prolific gooseberry, Ostheim cherry, and many old varieties too numerous to list.

As a young man, Milton also demonstrated an inventive and intellectually curious mind. He was fascinated by the concept of perpetual motion, that is, the notion that a mechanism could be essentially self-powered and operate indefinitely, requiring no additional external source of power. Although physicists have agreed for centuries that such mechanisms are impossible, violating the basic and well-established laws of thermodynamics, this mathematical riddle may have provided the impetus for one of Milton Hill's earliest inventions: A mouse-powered mousetrap.

This elaborate mouse trapping device was designed with three separate chambers, that baited, trapped, and, eventually, decapitated a mouse, all by means of spring-loaded entry ways that utilized the force exerted by the mouse as it entered each chamber.

Milton applied for and received patents in the U.S. and Canada, and had a prototype for his trap professionally built. Constructed within the confines of a fashionable raised-panel oak cabinet with multiple, vented hatches, the mechanism allowed for the trapping and dispatching of multiple mice. The separate chambers kept the objective of the device (and its accrual of victims) hidden from view for each succession of unsuspecting mice until it was too late, and escape was impossible.

Similar to his dreams of perpetual motion, Milton's ingenious mouse trap was entirely mouse-driven, and required no external efforts from the owner.

Being in no position to profitably manufacture the trap on his own, Milton attempted to sell his patented plans to manufacturers for the sum of $20,000. In a letter dated July 25, 1907, he described the operation of U.S. Patent No. 857,879:

"The device consists of a box-like body, comprising first a trap compartment, then a retaining compartment, and lastly a killing compartment. It is operated automatically by the animal, and a number of animals may be caught in succession without attention from the owner, as the trap is set by the animal passing from the first compartment into the retaining section.

The entrance to the trap is closed by sliding doors which are provided with operating arms. The doors are controlled by a platform, one end of which can be let down and held down by springs.

Milton J. Hill's elaborately designed, three-room mousetrap, ca. 1907, and his framed United States Patent. *Courtesy of Beth A. (Hill) Humma of Shire Valley Legacies and the Hill Family.*

When an animal enters the trap, the platform is released and closes the doors.

The animal finds a further opening into the second compartment, which is divided from the first by a swinging door. As soon as he passes through it [the] mechanism is released and the platform at the entrance returns to its former position, and the trap is ready for another visitor, the first being a prisoner in the second or retaining compartment. In its effort to find an exit, the animal will attempt to pass through the opening in the partition leading to the third compartment. The mere putting of its head through the small opening leading to the latter will cause it to come in contact with a depending plate, which hangs in front of the opening. A slight pressure against the plate moves a crank arm and other mechanisms and causes a sharp knife to descend, decapitating the animal. The knife is controlled by a spring and will perform its work very effectually...

The great possibilities for the sale of traps of this character, covering animals of all sizes and classes, will be apparent to all who have knowledge of the needs of this country in this respect..."[19]

It is perhaps fortunate that Milton's elaborate trap was never manufactured in the United States or Canada, and instead, he was able to focus his efforts on his true passion for painting.

On the day of November 6, 1910, Milton and Gertrude D. Strausser (1895-1978) were married. Their wedding took place in Bethlehem City, in Northampton County—which was at quite some distance from their home in those days—where their much beloved Lutheran Pastor Harry C. Kline had just relocated after serving for many years at Zion Union Church in Windsor Castle from 1897-1910.[20]

Gertie, as she was known in her youth,[21] was the daughter of John Reuben and Hettie Y. (Dreibelbis) Strausser of Shoemakersville. Born and raised on the farm of her grandparents Wilson and Mary Strausser, she grew up doing her share of the work along with her siblings, and developed a deep appreciation and skill for farming, caring for livestock, and gardening.

In 1910, when Gertrude married Milton and settled down on the Hill farm, she lived in the same small house with the extended Hill family, including her in-laws, John M. and Ellen E. Hill, her brother in-law John T. and his wife Catherine S. Hill, and her nephew Maurice J. Dries. In time, the farming duties shifted as John T. and his wife, Catherine S. Hill, moved to a property near Dreibelbis Station, and John M. and Ellen E. split the acreage with Milton and Gertrude, forty-six to thirty-four.

Eventually, when John and Ellen passed away in the 1930s, and Milton's career in painting continued to be a truly full-time endeavor, Gertrude managed the Hill family farm and its many operations, including the dairy, all of the acreage, and the livestock. In many ways, it was Gertrude who encouraged and fostered Milton's art, by managing the farm and allowing her husband the flexibility to fully utilize his creativity as an artist.

Above: Portrait of the young Milton J. Hill, ca. 1907. *Courtesy of Lee S. Heffner & Family.*

CHAPTER II

Painter of the Stars

Embodying a living tradition, barn star painters have graced the landscape of Southeastern Pennsylvania with their artistic presence for centuries. No one knows who the first artists were and precisely when they began to paint stars on the wooden siding of Pennsylvania barns. Like the Hill family, these earliest painters were indeed among the very same farmers, carpenters, builders, and tradesmen who established and sustained the agrarian communities of the region. The painting of the barn stars and other forms of rural decoration was likely to be only a secondary occupation which would serve to supplement an agricultural livelihood and add colorful expression to the folk culture of the Pennsylvania Dutch.[1]

Over time, the work of these earliest painters inspired the classic arrangements of stars and decorative borders that now characterize the rural landscape. Large and bold enough to be seen from across fields and valleys, barn stars appear in series across the facades and gable ends of barns and outbuildings, serving as focal points in the farmscapes of the region. These elaborate geometric murals, when paired together with decorative painted trim, accent otherwise quite ordinary agricultural structures, and elevate them beyond mere utility to the level of folk art.

Although the first artists kept no records or firsthand accounts of their work, and even their names are lost to the sands of time, their stories are preserved in the nineteenth-century barns which still stand proudly throughout the region. Little did they know that their work would one day capture the interest of people across the United States, and come to symbolize Pennsylvania Dutch culture as a whole.

Milton J. Hill began his career painting barn stars in 1902 at the age of 14 under the mentorship of his father, John M. Hill.[2] John was a professional painter, specializing in houses, barns, and even barn stars, although very little is known of

Above: Milton Hill's earliest remaining piece of artwork, painted on the Rausch Farm near Windsor Castle, Berks County. The star was repainted sometime in the late 1990s by local painter Donald I. Smith.
Opposite: Milton J. Hill painting his classic star pattern on the barn at the Hill Farm in Virginville ca. 1950. *Courtesy of the Pennsylvania Folklife Society Archive, Myrin Library, Ursinus College.*

29

Early hand-colored original photograph of the Rausch Farm in Windsor Castle, featuring the earliest known documentation of Milton Hill's signature barn star pattern. The photograph was taken circa 1912, and is one of the earliest properties that Milton Hill painted. *Courtesy of Allen Rausch & Family.*

his work. Some sources suggest that John's father Jacob M. Hill Jr. (b.1818) was also a barn painter, making Milton a third generation craftsman.[3] Initially, Milton worked as his father's assistant, and later when Milton became a master painter, his father worked under him well into the 1920s, creating a seamless continuation of the tradition in the family.

Sometime around 1910, Milton painted the very first star which would later become his signature pattern on the barn of Samuel Hepner in Windsor Castle, Berks County.[4] This "Hill Star," as it would later be known, was unlike anything else in the landscape up until that time, combining a repeating eight-pointed star pattern with an elaborate border of concentric circles and interlacing arcs of color gradients. His geometric composition was intricate and meticulous, and he combined high-contrast colors in the star points with subtle variations in the border. This created an optical, pulsating pattern that appeared to spin from a distance.

Milton's signature star was composed of ten colors. The star itself was black and yellow on a white background. Typically, concentric circles in three shades of red formed an interior border against interlacing arcs, in four shades of blue or green, for the outer border. The outer border colors were mixed in sequence by taking a true royal blue or a green composed of royal blue

A view of the forebay of the Rausch Barn, with Milton's signature stars, repainted by Donald I. Smith of Perry Township sometime in the late 1990s. *Survey of Decorated Barns, Patrick J. Donmoyer 2007-2020.*

and chrome yellow, and cutting it in equal proportions with white to form a secondary shade, and again with an equal amount of white paint for each successive layer in the border. The resulting gradient added a level of depth, producing a profound visual effect.

Shortly thereafter, Milton painted his signature stars on the barn of Daniel L. Smith (1840-1911), who had his newly painted barn photographed. This photograph is still at the farm, owned by Allen Rausch, whose great-grandfather Thomas purchased the farm in 1912. These stars were repainted sometime in the late 1990s by Donald I. Smith (1941-2014), a great-great-nephew of former owner Daniel Smith. The Rausch Barn is located just south of Windsor Castle.

Milton's first Hill Stars at the Samuel Hepner farm, later known as the Windsor Dairy, and even later the Kohler Ice Cream plant, had burned sometime after the year 2000, making the barn at the Rausch farm the earliest remaining Hill Stars still extant in the landscape today.

Although it is uncertain how many barns Milton Hill painted over the course of his long career, his work and legacy provided a continued folk-cultural narrative consistent with the experience of earlier generations. Milton asserted that his paintings were "stars"—*Schtanne* in his Pennsylvania Dutch mother tongue—artistic representations of the heavens.

While Milton's classic patterns were celestial in nature, depicting geometric stars with varying numbers of points, some designs in neighboring areas, such as the Lehigh Valley, are floral, featuring radial arrangements of lobed petals in organic patterns. These two types of motifs form the basic visual vocabulary of Pennsylvania's barn decorations, and parallel the original Pennsylvania Dutch words used to describe the artistic tradition.

Barn star patterns have been called a variety of names over the centuries, but two particular terms are predominant in the local vernacular.[5] These motifs have been called *Schtanne* (stars), a term descriptive of their angular, radial forms as abstract, geometric representations of heavenly bodies. Another name in Pennsylvania Dutch is *Blumme* (flowers), which identifies some of the very same geometry that is commonly found in the delicate blossoms of the terrestrial sphere.[6]

While these Pennsylvania Dutch ideas were predominant long before English terms came into common use, nevertheless, today the barn decorations are widely known as "hex signs"—an idea that did not originate among the Pennsylvania Dutch, but first appeared in tourism literature of the early twentieth century.[7] Travel journalists from outside the region promoted the spurious claim that the stars served the sole purpose

An early example of an early star by Milton J. Hill, repainted sometime in the late 1990s by Eric Claypoole of Lenhartsville. The barn once stood on Grandview Road, on the farm formerly belonging to Milton's school teacher Jeremiah P. Adam. Sadly the barn burned sometime around the year 2006. *Courtesy of Eric Claypoole.*

A scenic view of the Leiby Farm just outside of Virginville, Berks County, photographed in the 1960s by co-founder of the Kutztown Folk Festival Dr. Don Yoder, as a classic example of a Pennsylvania Dutch farmstead, complete with a decorated barn, a farmhouse, a range of outbuildings, meadows, woodlots, and acreage.
Don Yoder Collection, Pennsylvania German Cultural Heritage Center, Kutztown University.

of magical protection from the supernatural.[8] Although these accounts were highly imaginative and lacking any basis in fact, they were among the very first travelogues written about the decorated Pennsylvania barns, which served to introduce broad American audiences to the folk art of Pennsylvania.

Despite this confusion of the facts, barn stars of seemingly infinite variety, color, and form, tell an altogether different story of the vibrant artistic, agricultural, and spiritual traditions of the Pennsylvania Dutch. The stars were not expressions of "superstition" as the tourist literature suggested,[9] but abstract images of the heavens, refined by generations of artistic interest in geometry and agricultural interest in the stars. These beacons of celestial order and heralds of the annual progression of the seasons were once an essential part of the folk-cultural world view, and the inspiration for artistic expressions that permeated the material culture and architecture of Pennsylvania.[10]

Beginning sometime in the mid-nineteenth century, painting crews, under the direction of master painters, were responsible for painting the interiors of homes as well as barns, and the barn stars were part of the total package that was offered for the farm property.[11]

Milton Hill and his father operated under this very same model, employing family members and neighbors to help on painting jobs in the region. The availability of this hired work was subject to constant change, and their efforts were limited only to the hours that the agricultural seasons would permit.[12]

Above: One of two of the earliest known images of Milton Hill and his painting crew taken sometime around 1907 by Wallace A. Dietrich of Kutztown. It shows Milton Hill (far right) standing on a painter's platform suspended from the eaves with pulleys, along with his colleagues (left to right) Oscar (1869-1936) and Wilson Adam (1882-1936). The unknown owners standing in the barn yard are listed on the back of the photograph as members of the Stein Family. *Courtesy of Esther (Hill) Derr, daughter of Milton J. Hill*

Below: Another photograph by Wallace A. Dietrich, also attributed to members of the Stein family, located just outside Virginville. This was featured in the *Pennsylvania Dutchman* in February, 1953. *Pennsylvania Folklife Society, Myrin Library, Ursinus College.*

Although Milton showed a high degree of technical skill at an early age, his father paid him the same going-rate of ten cents per hour for his entry level work, and in addition, asked him to furnish his own paint.[13] This of course required Milton to learn the art of mixing his custom colors from linseed oil and commercial dry pigments, rather than rely on the costly ready-mixed "patent" paints that performed unpredictably even in the best of circumstances.

Unlike the painting crews of today, which are able to prepare and paint a barn with commercial paints in a matter of days, painting crews of the nineteenth century spent time making the paints as well as preparing the various surfaces that were to be painted. Although industrialized paint manufacturing had made considerable progress since the advent of large-scale production in the mid-nineteenth century, commercial paints did not even enter into the equation for barn star painters such as Milton's father John. Instead, painters preferred to purchase pigments locally or order them from national distributors. The pigments were mixed by hand with boiled linseed oil for exterior paints, or milk-based casein paints for interiors. In fact, some artists mixed their own paints well into the twentieth century, knowing that their tried-and-true recipes were likely to outlast anything purchased commercially.[75]

By 1907, Milton Hill had formed his own three-man painting crew with Oscar (1869-1936) and Wilson Adam (1882-1936), two cousins originally from Temple, Berks County.[15] Oscar owned and operated the successful Meadow Farm, which was the first dairy in Windsor Township to produce bottled milk before the First World War.[16] Two early photographs by photographer Wallace A. Dietrich (1853-1909) of Kutztown capture Milton's painting crew in action at two separate locations. In one photo (opposite page, below), the three men stand on a painter's suspended platform after a day's work on the Daniel Stein barn between Virginville and Moselem. The stars are only partially finished above the painters on the siding of the barn's extended forebay, and the photo reveals the painting process. The center of the star is unfinished, and the new white background was not painted as a solid coat, but cut into the space between the star points. The family of Daniel Stein stands proudly below the barn, along with their team of draft horses. Their herd of dairy cows stands in the barnyard.

Another early photograph by Wallace A. Dietrich (above) shows the same three painters standing suspended on their platform, with Milton wearing solid white coveralls. The stars are not yet fully painted, but the interlaced border of Milton's signature star is complete. Both photographs were taken approximately a year or so before Dietrich moved his photography business

Above: Detail of Milton's Hill's three-person painting crew, circa 1907. Milton is wearing the white coveralls. Pennsylvania German Cultural Heritage Center, Kutztown University. Gift of Harold & Esther (Hill) Derr & Family.

from Kutztown to Allentown, and then passed away in the summer of 1909.[17]

Over time, Milton employed a number of local people as members of his crew including his daughter Ellen's husband Stanley O. Heffner (1916-1999); his brother-in-law Paul Hoffa (b. 1897), husband of Gertrude's sister Sallie D. (Strausser) Hoffa (1889-1982); and Milton Berstler (1891-1966), brother of Cass S. (Catherine Berstler) Hill (1902-1959), the wife of Milton's brother John Tyburtis Hill. Over a dozen others appear in Milton's ledger, including Elmer D. Adam (1892-1969), Curtin Heckman (1889-1951), Charles Guldin, Robert Yoder, George Schappell, Walter Moyer, John Dreibelbis, and George Keim.

Milton would later recall that during these early years of his painting career, each barn took a little over one week for three of them to paint, and each of the stars took Milton about eight hours to complete with two coats of paint.[18] The four shades of blue in Milton's border were mixed by cutting each successive shade in half with white paint to produce a monochromatic gradient.

Like previous generations of painters, most of Milton's trade secrets were learned on the job, and were rarely recorded. No ledgers of barn star painters from the nineteenth century are known to exist, leaving us to merely speculate on the particulars of time, materials, and process employed to decorate a barn in the early days. Milton's work ledger is unusual, however, in the fact that he maintained meticulous accounts in his first few decades of painting, and it is one of the only known ledgers of its kind to survive to the present day. Milton's ledger outlined and itemized his hourly project schedules, the names of all of the various members of his painting crews, the names of his clients, itemized lists of paint pigments, and, in one instance, precisely how long it took him to paint the stars a barn.

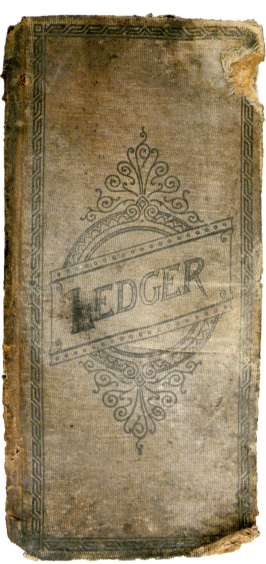

In 1912, Milton Hill and his brother-in-law Paul Hoffa spent 411¾ hours **collectively** to paint a house, a barn, and a series of stars on the barn of George Hoch. This is likely George K. Hoch (1860-1948), who operated a farm in nearby Richmond Township, and is buried at Zion Moselem Church.[19] According to his ledger entry from 1912, Hill painted the house and barn from May 23 to June 8 and, beginning on June 10, he spent 10 ¼ hours starting the series of stars. On June 11 and 12, Hill and his assistant each put in 22 hours painting the stars, for a total of 52 ¼ hours. After 42 additional hours for cleanup and finishing

Above: Milton Hill's Ledger, showing two hourly accounts of working along with Paul Hoffa to paint stars at the farm of George Hoch, near Kutztown on Crystal Cave Road. The hours expended for the stars are labeled.

Opposite: The cover of Milton's ledger, documenting his early career painting houses and barns from 1907-1922. *Pennsylvania German Cultural Heritage Center, Kutztown University. Gift of Harold & Esther (Hill) Derr & Family.*

work on the barn, the job was complete. Hill was paid 15 cents per hour, and his partner only 10 cents, with each of them receiving a total amount of $30.90 and $20.57 for 206 and 205 ¾ hours respectively!

Although adjustment for inflation suggests that their wages would be worth a combined total of $1,300 today,[20] it is still easy to see that labor was comparatively inexpensive in those days, allowing for artists to produce colorful barn paintings at rates far below the labor of today. The painters were compensated only $7.03 for the painting of the stars, which amounts to an adjusted $182.43 in today's currency. If Milton painted a total of 4 stars on the barn (an average in his immediate community in Virginville), each star would have been valued at $1.75 each.

The inexpensive nature of this form of art made it easily within the means of farmers of moderate income. Milton Hill

Ephemera from Milton Hill's painting and paper-hanging business, including a house-painting invoice from 1922, wallpaper samples, and business cards from four different periods of his painting career.
Gift of Esther (Hill) & Harold Derr, and Courtesy of Lee S. Heffner & Family.

Milton Hill on a painting job sometime in the 1940s with his painting crew, consisting of (left to right) son-in-law Stanley O. Heffner, and sons Jacob W., and Milton D. *Courtesy of Lee S. Heffner & Family.*

recommended that his stars be repainted every ten years or so, allowing for a steady flow of work during the decades that he painted throughout the region.

When Milton's sons, John Lewis (1911-1963), Jacob Wilson (1912-1991), and Milton Daniel Hill (1918-2008), were old enough to help, they also served as crucial members of this painting crew, as well as his son-in-law Stanley O. Heffner (1916-1999). Together they not only painted barns and houses, they also specialized in wall-paper, patterned graining, stenciling, and other specialty jobs for house interiors. Milton also served as a wall-paper dealer, who ordered the materials in bulk, and kept samples in his ledger for placing custom orders. Although Milton's decorative interior work ranged all over Northern Berks, and even in the city of Reading, few of these jobs were documented to show the degree of his professional skill.

Although the barn stars probably occupied only a small portion of his time as a painter, they served as a unique form of public advertisement for his services. Examples of his stars have been located on barns throughout Virginville, Windsor Castle, Hamburg, Kempton, Lenhartsville, Kutztown, Fleetwood, Moselem, and the surrounding area.

Throughout his life as a master painter, Milton's process was methodical and precise. Along with his common painting tools, he carried the tools of a draftsman, consisting of compass dividers of various sizes, trammel-points, straight edges, squares, and scribes. Each star was scribed directly into the wood, creating cleanly divided edges for each color area in the design. This technique allowed him to maximize his time and effort, by providing straight score-marks to guide the edge of his brush. Milton also occasionally used patterns, composed of metal shapes cut from tin that were backed with leather, which formed a pad that would not slide against the surface of the barn siding.[21]

Like other barn star painters of his time, Milton's techniques of permanently scribing the wood with his geometric layout allowed him to repaint his stars every decade or so as needed, simply by following his scribe lines. In addition, this effect was also enhanced by a process called differential solar weathering, whereby the rays of the sun cause a painted surface to erode. This takes place when barn stars are exposed to the elements, and the interaction between the rays of the sun and the surface of the wood produces a very pronounced visual relief over the course of a few decades. Areas of wooden siding which are protected by multiple coats of paint or more resilient pigments tend to weather more slowly than areas with less protection. Gradually, over time, this creates the appearance of an ephemeral relief —sometimes called a "ghost"— that allows for the old geometric designs to be distinctly visible, even when painted over with a solid color.[22]

This weathering process was helpful to Milton, who was able to use the "ghost" effect to his advantage and repaint his designs without having to expend the effort to re-scribe the geometric layout. Certain low sun angles of the early morning and late afternoon produce a raking light that causes weathered star patterns to quite visibly emerge from the siding, and later disappear from sight when the sun's angle changes—giving this weathering effect its name.

While some observers have assumed that the barn star "ghosts" are intentionally carved or etched, they are not. Instead, the relief is produced over time by the natural weathering power of the sun. This effect encouraged some of the subsequent generations of barn painters to repaint historic barn stars using the ghosts

Above: This weathered, sixteen-pointed barn star is one of a series from a barn in Windsor Castle, Berks County, attributed to Milton Hill who painted extensively in the immediate area. These stars were likely painted in the early twentieth century, but show patterns of highly pronounced relief, produced by the sun's weathering of the wooden barn siding.
Bottom: A weathered barn star "ghost," salvaged from the wagon shed from the same farm in Windsor Castle, Berks County. Barn stars weather in the elements, and the interaction between the rays of the sun and the surface of the wood produces a pronounced relief over the course of many years. This relief is produced unintentionally by a process called differential solar weathering, and it is still visible even if the star is painted over. *Pennsylvania German Cultural Heritage Center, Kutztown University. Gift of Bart W. Hill, great-grandson of Milton J. Hill.*

as templates for restoration. This allowed them to maintain the local aesthetics of the landscape, while exploring up-close the geometric layouts of previous artists, whose works were emblazoned on the surface of the wooden barn siding.

One of the most unusual ghosts attributed to Milton Hill, was formerly located just south of Windsor Castle, where four sixteen-pointed star bursts were arranged across the forebay of the barn, and a large thirty-two-pointed star adorned the gable end of a wagon shed facing the road. Although the designs were not Milton's signature pattern, the complex geometry has led some local people to attribute the work to him. Milton painted a wide variety of patterns in addition to his classic Hill Star, although many of these designs are not well documented.

While it is unknown precisely how many barns Milton painted over the course of his life, his career as a professional barn painter lasted over fifty years—a staggering statistic which stands as a testament to his prolific and hard-working artistic lifestyle.

Milton Hill was a humble and introverted artist who spent far more of his time painting than self-promoting or debating, but he certainly became impassioned when he defended his work against those who called his stars "hex signs" and presumed them to have a supernatural significance. Milton had been painting for decades before this phrase was introduced to the region by tourist literature.[23] Milton deeply resented that his work, and the work of fellow artists in the region, was subjected to this interpretation.

Nevertheless, he tended to be an unassuming man by nature, and even resisted the title of "artist," calling his son John L. Hill "the artist of the family" because he painted farmscape scenes of livestock on local barns.[79] Hill referred to himself as a "barn decorator" and painter of "various star patterns"—suggesting that he was merely a technician, as opposed to the creative genius that he really was.

In fact, were it not for Milton Hill's public appearance at the Kutztown Folk Festival, and the promotion of his work to a national audience, he might have remained only a local personality with limited influence on the tradition as a whole. Instead, Folk Festival director Alfred L. Shoemaker, together with his coworker Olive G. Zehner, recognized the importance of Hill's work, and courted him for several years before he finally agreed to attend the Kutztown Folk Festival to demonstrate his art. This put Milton into the national spotlight as the foremost barn painter of the twentieth century, and this encounter with the Festival staff launched the evolution of painting barn stars on commercial signboard as a modern manifestation of a folk tradition.

Above: Milton Hill's original compass, used for scribing the interlacing arcs of his intricate borders for his signature Hill Star pattern. The compass shows evidence of having been repaired after decades of use. *Pennsylvania German Cultural Heritage Center, Kutztown University. Gift of Harold & Esther (Hill) Derr & Family.*

Gertrude D. (Strausser) and Milton J. Hill standing by the barnyard fence in front of the Hill family barn, decorated with Milton's signature star patterns, circa 1950. The humor in this picture is partially due to the fact that Gertrude was considerably shorter than Milton, and stood on a bucket for the staging of this photograph. Together the pair raised three sons and two daughters, and were married for over 61 years. *Courtesy of Beth A. (Hill) Humma, & Shire Valley Legacies.*

CHAPTER III

Gertrude D. Hill & The Family Farm

At the same time that Milton pursued his successful painting career, his wife, Gertrude D. (Strausser) Hill, operated and managed the dairy farm, which was the family's primary source of income and sustenance. All the while, she cared for their five children, cooked all the meals, cleaned the house, planted and tended extensive gardens and fruit trees, milked their herd of dairy cows twice a day, fed and cared for the pigs, sheep, chickens, and ducks, and orchestrated all the work of the extended family and friends who gladly assisted with the acreage in the yearly planting, harvesting, and hay-making.[1]

Gertrude Hill began her work on the Hill farm at the age of fifteen, when she married Milton in 1910. By the time Milton's parents passed away in the 1930s, she had already become the chief bread-winner of the family, a role that she maintained well into the 1960s, when the Hill farm still operated as a multi-generational family farm. Children and grandchildren, nieces and nephews, all played roles in sustaining the farm operation, and Gertrude was the magnanimous soul of the Hill Farm, who kept the family together.

According to the Pennsylvania Triennial Farm Census of 1927, Gertrude and Milton's farming operation, situated on 34 acres of land in Perry Township, did not emphasize the cultivation of grain or other crops like their neighbors, but instead focused on the raising of livestock. In that year, with only three acres of hay, they supported 2 horses, 5 milk cows, 2 heifers, 20 pigs and 2 sows for breeding, 75 laying hens, and 25 broiler chickens. The land also supported 15 apple trees and a single pear tree.[2]

Due to the fact that the 1927 farm census was taken at a time of rapid change in the use of technology, the enumerators also tracked changes in the adoption of modern amenities. The Hill farm is listed as having no running water in the kitchen, no electricity, no furnace heating system, no milking machines, no silos, one automobile, but no tractors, trucks, or gas engines, and no telephones or radios. It was not until 1943 that Milton and Gertrude's youngest daughter Esther paid for the installation of a bathroom in the house by herself at the age of sixteen, using her wages from working in the undergarment factory in Shoemakersville.

The original star on the gable end of the barn at the Hill Homestead, first painted by Milton J. Hill, and later repainted by his sons John L. and Jacob W. Hill. *Courtesy of Pennsylvania's Americana Region.*

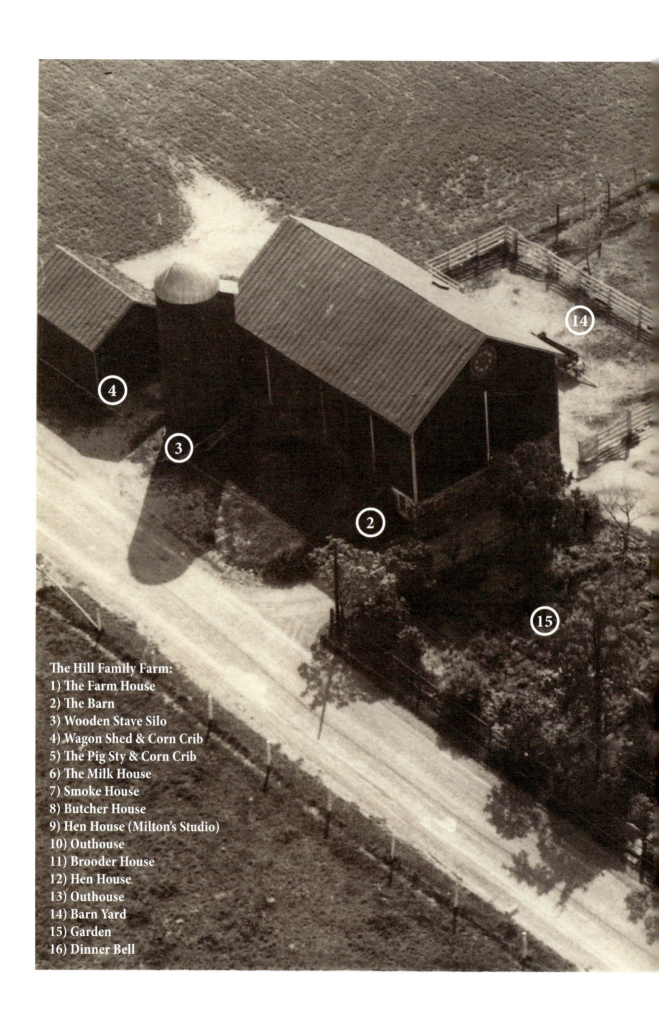

The Hill Family Farm:
1) The Farm House
2) The Barn
3) Wooden Stave Silo
4) Wagon Shed & Corn Crib
5) The Pig Sty & Corn Crib
6) The Milk House
7) Smoke House
8) Butcher House
9) Hen House (Milton's Studio)
10) Outhouse
11) Brooder House
12) Hen House
13) Outhouse
14) Barn Yard
15) Garden
16) Dinner Bell

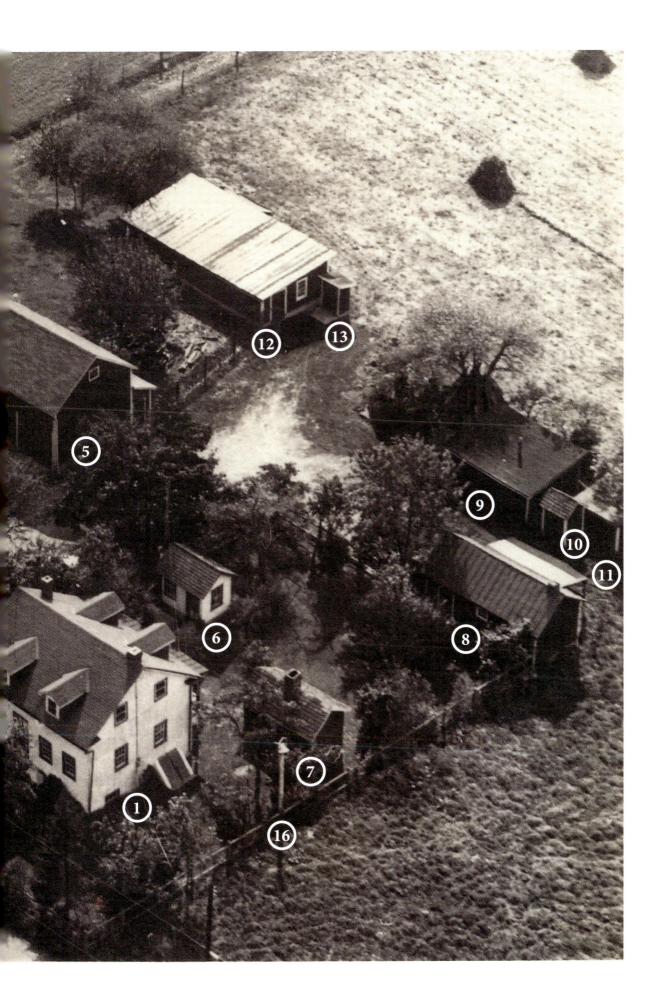

Gertrude Hill and her granddaughter, Dorian, daughter of Harold and Esther (Hill) Derr, ca. 1955. *Courtesy of Beth A. (Hill) Humma & Shire Valley Legacies.*

Also included in the 1927 farm census was Milton's father, John M. Hill, who rented the adjacent farm acreage, consisting of 46 acres, where a total of 23 acres were in crop production, including 10 acres of corn, 5 acres of wheat, 6 acres of oats, and 2 acres of potatoes, as well as 12 apple trees, 4 peach trees, and 5 pear trees. With 7 acres of hay, John supported 3 milk cows, 8 pigs, 75 laying hens, and 25 broilers. Interestingly, the census indicates that John owned no horses or mules, and had no tractor, suggesting that he shared the same draft animals as the primary farm, and cooperated with the rest of the family to work the land to the documented degree of productivity. It was also essential that John and Gertrude shared resources between the two operations in order to support the family, as they all lived in the same small, story-and-a-half stone farm house.

The farm layout was situated along the Virginville Road (formerly called R.D. 2), with some acreage on the north and south sides. The barn and other farm buildings, were on the south side, and the property extended to a branch of the Maidencreek.[3] The farm was a classic Pennsylvania Dutch farmstead including a large forebay barn from the late nineteenth century. The barn was banked against the Virginville Road, with a modern milkhouse and a wooden silo on the east side, as well as a long farm lane that led from the barn to the pasture bordering the creek. The barnyard stood directly south of the forebay side of the barn, and was enclosed with a white fence. Sharing this border of the barnyard was a sizable piggery with a corncrib on the south side, and beyond this stood a large chicken house for the laying hens.[4]

Above: The Schappell Farm Family, who lived on the neighboring original Hill farm next to Milton and Gertrude's 80+ acre farm. Left to right: Son, Albert M. (1895-1961); daughter, Eva M. (1907-1989); son, James M. (1897-1971); mother, Margaret S. (Mengel) (1869-1933), and father, Sassaman J. Schappell (1872-1959). Sister and brother, Eva and James, were good neighbors and friends of the Hill family, and continued to operate the farm next door for many years. *Courtesy of Lee S. Heffner & Family.*

Below: Gertrude D. (Strausser) Hill's parents John R. Strausser (1869-1952) and Hettie Y. (Dreibelbis) Strausser (1871-1945). *Courtesy of Lee S. Heffner & Family.*

The Hill barn and silo, with the milkhouse bordering the fenced-in barn yard. A corn crib stands to the right, and the gable of the farm house is visible on the far left. *Courtesy of Lee S. Heffner & Family.*

Along the west side of the barn, a short farm lane divided the barnyard from the large gardens and fruit trees surrounding the stone farmhouse. A dinner bell stood next to the house to the west, alongside a bakeoven and smokehouse, under which their faithful old dog Chupy slept. An old spring-fed milkhouse stood next to the old stone-lined well and pump. To the south lay a butcher shop with a double-kettle butchering stove, and another chicken house for brooding hens, which was later converted to Milton's painting studio. There were two outhouses, and one was added during the depression through a public sanitation project through a local WPA project.[5]

This farm complex, with each of its specialized spaces and buildings, was an excellent example of the gradually evolving Pennsylvania farmscape, which not only supported profitable, diversified farming operations, but especially furnished the sustenance of a large family needed to work and maintain the farm.

Gertrude took pride in the cleanliness of her farm, and kept a firm routine. Gertrude woke each morning at 4 o'clock to milk her dairy cows by hand. Even when her son-in-law, Harold J. Derr, later bought her two automated milking machines, she wouldn't use them, preferring instead the technique she'd employed since her youth. Gertrude would bend over at the waist, rest her shoulder and head against each animal's flank, and work the udder by hand, keeping rhythm by moving her jaw from side to side with the effort. Family members recall that she could fill a pail with milk faster than anyone they knew. She kept her milking parlor spotless, and whitewashed it herself to keep it fresh. The windowsills were finished with concrete moldings that resembled those of a house interior, and she kept potted red geraniums on each sill, where they drank up the morning sun.

Gertrude's modernized milking parlor with ample windows along the front stable wall, poured concrete drains, and metal stanchions was part of a major renovation to the Hill farm in compliance with the Department of Agriculture's sanitation laws in the 1940s. Milton and Gertrude's

Above: Milton, Esther, and Gertrude Hill standing in the yard at the Hill family farm ca. 1944, when she was 17 years old. Esther would later go on to help her father paint his barn stars on sign board. *Courtesy of Beth A. (Hill) Humma & Shire Valley Legacies.*

Below: The three Strausser sisters (left to right), Mabel (Strausser) Hinnershitz, Sallie (Strausser) Hoffa, and Gertrude (Strausser) Hill. *Courtesy of Beth A. (Hill) Humma & Shire Valley Legacies.*

Gertrude's milk cows, grazing in the field to the west of the farm house. *Courtesy of Lee S. Heffner & Family.*

oldest son John L. Hill, a skilled contractor and carpenter, was instrumental in these renovations. It was at this time that the forebay of the barn was filled in with cinderblock, large windows were added, and a fully-compliant, modern milk house was built at the southeast corner of the barn.

Immediately following the morning milking and storing of the milk in the cooled milkhouse, Gertrude would take any milk past its prime, and generously feed it to the farm cats in a big trough in the barn yard. When she shouted "Pood-lah! Pood-lah! Pood-lah!"[6] the cats would come running from their hiding places in the barn to drink up the milk.

By 6 o'clock, Gertrude would bring a scuttle of coal from the basement to stoke the cookstove, and serve Milton his breakfast, which was the same every morning: two dippy-eggs,[7] toast, a bowl of home-canned peaches, and coffee.

Following breakfast, she would recruit the children (and later the grandchildren) for gathering the eggs, and setting the cows out to pasture in the lower fields. She then made sure the animals were fed, and performed the umpteen daily chores necessary on the farm, including tending and harvesting the productive vegetable garden; canning and preserving the vegetables and fruit for the winter; baking; doing the wash; butchering and cleaning chickens; and scheduling all the necessary tasks with the family work-force, such as cutting and bringing in the hay, mending fences, and breeding their 18 cows with the bull they maintained on-site.

In the evening, before ringing the dinner bell to gather the whole family in for supper, she called in the cows from the pasture yelling "Hepp da!" (giddy-up there!) and put them back in the barn for feeding. Before dark, the chicken coop was secured with the hens safe inside. After dinner, she milked the cows again, and stored the milk in the milkhouse.

When each day had finally come to a close, and every person and creature on the farm was fed and contented, she would walk to the tree swing hanging from the old maple tree along the path back to the farm house by the garden, and would sit for a long moment in solitude. The swing faced her gardens, where something was always blooming from spring to the first hard frost in the fall.

Along a pathway between the house, a grape arbor stretched, and lilac bushes in deep and pale purple, crimson, and white edged the garden and fence along Virginville Road, filling the yard with their fragrance.

Gertrude's love of color spread throughout the garden, where crocuses, daffodils, hyacinths, peonies, lily of the valley, irises, phlox, bleeding hearts, and lilies ushered in the spring. Daisies, daylilies, asters, black-eyed Susans, gladiolus, hostas, hibiscus, and sunflowers thrived throughout the heat of summer. The chrysanthemums held the final watch in fall before the frosts would lull the garden to sleep for the winter.[8]

Sour cherry trees bordered the barn, and fruit trees of all kinds were situated in the yard and within the fence of the garden. Pears, apples, cherries, persimmons, quince, peaches, and apricots, along with strawberries from the garden, provided the ample produce for making jams, jellies, preserves, and canning. Nuts were gathered from trees along the edges of the fields and shelled by hand, especially black walnuts and hickory nuts.

Her vegetable garden consisted of a series of raised earth beds, that were carefully maintained, and bordered by packed earth pathways. Her seasonal vegetables included onions, peas, green stringbeans, yellow wax beans, brussels sprouts, carrots, white winter radishes, asparagus, tomatoes, lettuce, and, of course, cabbage, to be made into sauerkraut.

Always complete with her apron sewn from cloth chicken-feed bags, Gertrude knew how to make the best use of the resources on the farm. Having lived through the era of the Great Depression, she wasted nothing, and even lovingly sewed shirts and other clothing for her children and grandchildren from feed bags to match her apron.

Gertrude carried a small ledger in her apron pocket for notes, recipes, and quick reference. The ledger was contained within a book of useful information issued each year by the Griffith & Boyd Company of Baltimore, Maryland, which specialized in the distribution of natural and synthetic fertilizers. As a courtesy to customers, the ledger contained tables of information for farm and household use, including how to calculate quantities of seed per acre, methods to measure quantities of corn in the crib and grain in the granary, forms for farming contracts, as well as copious treatments for illness among livestock, and other useful household remedies and instructions. Gertrude filled the blank pages with recipes of her favorite cakes, breads, and desserts, and she kept the additional contents for reference and practical use.

Detail of the beautifully formed windowsills of Gertrude Hill's old milking parlor, which she regularly whitewashed, and adorned with potted red geraniums.

Gertrude's practicality was not only an essential part of her work ethic, it was also borne out of the necessity from her years caring for the family, both young and old, as well as the animals upon which the family depended. Gertrude served as the family's first line of defense in cases of mild illness, and even dabbled with dentistry when the

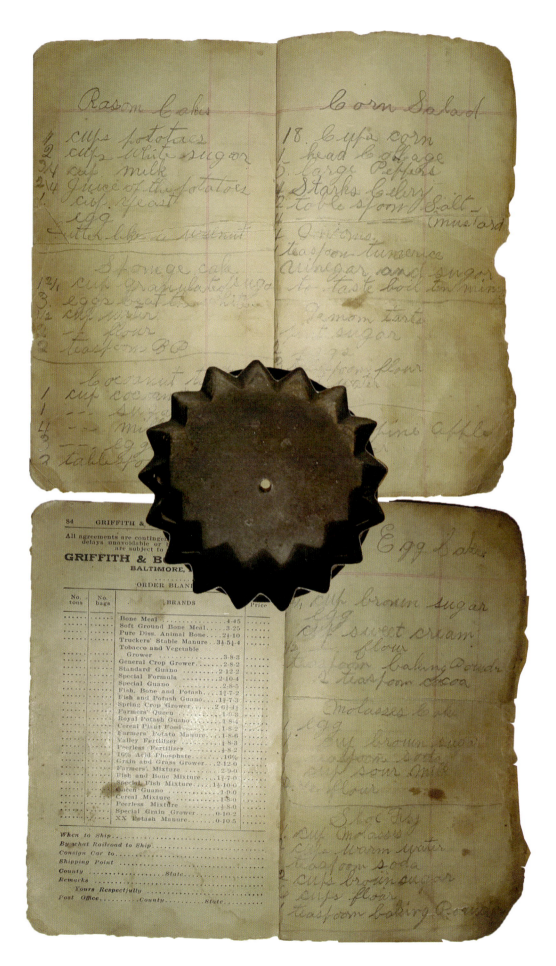

Above: Four generations of the Hill Family, left to right: Great granddaughter Valerie E. Fry, oldest daughter Ellen E. (Hill) Heffner, Gertrude D. (Strausser) Hill, and granddaughter Mabel M. (Heffner) Fry. *Courtesy of Betty J. (Heffner) Mengel & Family.*

occasion called for it. Her grandchildren later recalled that "Granny" knew old remedies for fevers, infected hangnails, and upset stomachs. She would even pull loose teeth when the need arose, with nothing but a clean hanky and her strong grip.

As Gertrude's five children grew up, they too were raised with the realities and benefits of farm work. When the three sons John L., Jacob W., and Milton D. grew to adulthood, they were eventually employed under their father Milton for his painting work, while their sister Ellen Elizabeth (1914-2004) remained on the farm and assisted her mother in the farm work. In particular, she helped with her younger sister, Esther, who was born in 1927, when she was almost thirteen years old. Esther, who was the youngest, and last of Gertrude and Milton's children, had a special bond with her older sister Ellen, who essentially raised her, while their mother managed the dairy operation, and cared for the eleven-person, multi-generational household.

Eventually, Milton's parent's had both passed away in the 1930s, and the two oldest sons got married and left the family farm to pursue other work. John L. and Jacob W. married two sisters, Melva Viola Brobst (1912-1985), and Agnes Anna Isabella Brobst (1914-1993). John and Melva lived in the converted one-room Gruber's School House in Perry Township. John was a skilled carpenter and continued to nurture his painting work. He developed a keen interest in complementing his father's barn stars with murals of livestock and farm scenes, many of which can still be seen along the Virginville

Opposite: Gertrude Hill's pocket cookbook and farm guide, with manuscript recipes for shoofly pie, molasses cake, corn salad, fasnachts, and other traditional favorites, with one of her old tin cookie cutters in the shape of a star. *Courtesy of Dorian Derr Fetherolf & Family.*

Family photograph of four generations of the extended Hill and Strausser Family, taken in 1952. Top row, left to right: John M., Milton D., Jacob W., Agnes A. I. (Brobst), Harold J. Derr, Stanley O. Heffner, Melva V. (Brobst), John L., William T. and Daniel T. Middle row, left to right: Anna E., June R. (Schappell), Gertrude D. (Strausser), Esther L. (Hill) Derr and baby daughter Dorian L., Ellen E. (Hill) Heffner, Milton J., Mary G., and Mabel M. Heffner. Front row, left to right: Robert M., Patricia I., Carol S., Betty J. Heffner, and her twin brother, Lee S. Heffner. *Courtesy of Lee S. Heffner & Family.*

Road. Jacob W. went into business with his mother Gertrude's younger brother Warren D. Strausser (1905-1983) with trucking and manufacturing of truck trailers and beds, called Hill & Strausser, and later took his business to Water Street in nearby Shoemakersville, retitling the business Hill Manufacturing.

On October 29, 1936, Ellen E. (1914-2004) married Stanley O. Heffner (1916-1999), who took up residence at the Hill farm, and worked for Milton as part of his painting crew. Their oldest daughter Mabel M. was born at the homestead on May 10, 1937. Ellen and Stanley continued to live and work at the Hill Farm until they eventually moved to the neighboring farm, where their twins Betty Jane and Lee Stanley were born on December 22, 1944.

Gertrude's grandson Lee recalls growing up amidst the collective spirit of farming, working alongside family, friends and neighbors, all carefully orchestrated under Gertrude's management:

> Grandmother Gertrude Hill scheduled the day-long silo filling work each year in late summer during the 1950's. This was, indeed, a community effort since the Hill farm did not own any silo filling equipment.
>
> Loyal neighbors came together to pitch in for this annual service. Just a short distance west of the Hill farm, dairy farmers including the Stanley Miller and the James Adam families contracted to fill the thirty-foot wood stave silo for Milton and Gertrude Hill. My grandmother was always punctual in selecting the optimal time for the corn harvest which fed her dairy cows for the coming winter. Mature corn with succulent green fodder produced the top grade of silage. I can still visualize the oozing liquid running out at the base of the silo's concrete perimeter as the fermentation process began and continued for several days.
>
> Within three to five days, the filled silo was topped with tar paper to minimize spoilage. Grandfather Milton Hill and I completed this job together.

Bank side view of the Hill barn along the Virginville Road, with the wooden stave silo situated on the east end of the building. *Courtesy of Lee S. Heffner & Family.*

As was common in a rural community, the farmhouse became a treasure because of a sumptuous noon meal prepared by Gertrude and her daughters, Ellen (Hill) Heffner (my mother) and Esther (Hill) Derr.

Wooden boards were added to the expanded dinner table to accommodate the number of hungry workers who craved the Hill-style meal for many years. The menu included ham, chicken, filling, corn, green beans, applesauce, jellies, bread, assorted desserts including cakes and pies, and of course coffee and water.

Another very memorable happening on silo filling day that the neighboring farmers enjoyed tremendously was Gertrude's homemade lemonade! She possessed a "mental recipe" for this heavenly mixture with the proper balance of orange and lemon slices, sugar and water, all blended into a large metal bucket, complete with ice cubes.

I still visualize my grandmother leaving the farmhouse with this tasty treat as she walked the south perimeter of the garden fence toward the driveway between the garden and the west end of the barn to the back of the barn's north side to the silo filling scene in order to offer the lemonade to the hard-working, sweating crew. Talk about a rejuvenating treat! The lemonade was ladled from a metal dipper into individual cups for the thirsty workers.

Every neighborly worker knew their assigned job in this silo filling event. The Miller family and the Adam family brought their harvester, blower and piping that was set up along side the silo. I remember that James Adam generally used his Oliver 77 tractor for belt power to the blower which hoisted the silage to the top of the silo, then down inside to its destination.

This entire project began soon after each farmer's own morning chores were completed, with their arrival at the Hill farm between 8:00-8:30 a.m. When the silo filling was completed, Gertrude paid each helper a more than fair wage for their service, allowing of course, the required renumeration for the farm machinery that was supplied (tractors, wagons, silo filler, etc).

In the evening of this completed work, I would reflect upon this beautiful example of true farm community spirit, care, and friendship!

Lee Heffner eventually lived and worked at the Hill farm following his graduation from high school between 1962 and 1964,

Diagrams of the Hill Farm's equipment fleet used by Gertrude Hill and her grandson Lee Heffner, consisting of a McCormick-Deering Farmall F-14 tractor and No. 9 sicklebar mower; and an F-20 tractor and New Holland Model 77 Automatic Pick-up Baler with a Wisconsin air-cooled engine. The Hill's tractors used rubber tires. Illustrations from McCormick-Deering *Instruction Books F-14 & F20*; McCormick-Deering *Serviceman's Guide*; and New Holland *Assembling and Operating Instructions Model 77*.

Bales of hay from *die Hoiet* lie in the east hay field at the Hill family farm in 1959. *Courtesy of Lee S. Heffner & Family.*

and worked alongside Gertrude milking cows, cutting hay, mending fences, and supporting all aspects of the farm operation with his Grandmother. One single aspect of the farm work that Gertrude left to others was driving the McCormick-Deering F-14 tractor, which Lee used for preparing the land, cutting, harvesting, and hauling. Even with the availability of this powerful machine, many of the implements were left over from the days of draft-animal powered operations on the Hill Farm.

This was especially true during *die Hoiet* and *die Ohmet*, the primary and secondary hay cutting seasons. The old McCormick-Deering sickle bar mower, which was used for cutting the timothy and alfalfa for the cows, was only 5' wide with steel wheels, and was gear-driven, rather than operated with a power take off shaft. While Lee drove the tractor, Gertrude sat on the high metal seat of the mower, where formerly the driver of the draft horses sat, and she operated the raising and lowering of the sickle bar by hand with a lever. When Gertrude was no longer able to assist with the mowing, Lee enlisted his Aunt Esther to operate the sickle bar. Gertrude also later paid her granddaughter Dorian $2.50 per field to fill in.

Lee baled the hay with the New Holland 77 baler pulled by the powerful McCormick-Deering F-20 tractor. Since the Hill relatives had day employment, bales were dropped on the hay field, waiting for late afternoon or evening pick-up. When the relatives came to help, the bales were stacked on the hay wagon pulled by the F-14 tractor, and driven to the upper story of the barn for storage.

In earlier days, hay was picked up loose with a New Idea hay-loader attached to the hay wagon. After the filled wagon was pulled into the barn's upper story, the loose hay was distributed into the mow with the hay track that ran just under the ridge of

A view of the end grain of a saddle-notched, hewn log repurposed as a movable support in the overden of the Hill family barn. The presence of this log suggests that an earlier log structure once stood on the site of the Hill homestead. This remnant could perhaps have come from an original log crib barn, a log home, or a log outbuilding of which nothing but this log remains. The current Hill barn was built in the second half of the nineteenth century, making the possibility that a log barn preceded it very likely.

the barn roof. A large fork, operated with a rope, hoisted the hay from the wagon up to the rafters, where the trolley carried the load along the track to the end of the barn where it was released into the mow. Later, once the baler was introduced to the farm, a hay elevator powered by an electric motor carried the bales to where they were stored in the hay mow on either end of the barn.

The old Hill barn had two mows for hay and straw, and two wagon bays. The upper story of the barn had remained virtually unchanged since its construction in the second half of the nineteenth century - all except for the removal of the low partition walls formerly used with threshing, so that baled hay could be more easily loaded with an open floor plan.

High above, and only accessible with the built-in hay ladders, lay the lateral beams of the overden, used for overhead storage. These movable beams were recycled from a log structure that likely once stood on the property, and showed the corner saddle-notches used in the construction of some of the earliest buildings in the region. These quiet reminders of early settlement may have been the original log walls of the Hill homestead, or an earlier log crib barn.

The Hill farm remained in Gertrude's capable hands for decades, and the homestead remained a center of life for the extended family, as even her grandchildren grew up and had families of their own. As Milton's career as a painter continued to thrive, so too did Gertrude's farming operation continue to support the family through many transitions and changes over the years. Gertrude's meticulous work ethic and attention to detail paralleled her husband's artistic precision and inventive spirit. Indeed Gertrude's support and dedication to Milton was a true gift of domestic and family stability which allowed his barn star painting career to flourish and revolutionize the traditional art form.

Interior framing of the Hill barn from the second half of the nineteenth century, showing hay mows, wagon bays, and (in the foreground) the lateral beams of the overden used for overhead storage.
Survey of Decorated Barns, Patrick J. Donmoyer 2007-2020.

A view of the extended forebay of the Leiby barn, located between Virginville and Lenhartsville, that was painted by Milton Hill. This barn was one of many publicly visible barns throughout the region that appeared in publications advocating for tourism in the region. *Courtesy of the Pennsylvania Folklife Society, Ursinus College.*

CHAPTER IV

Magical Misconceptions

With the advent of the automobile in the early twentieth century, tourists from across the Mid-Atlantic traveled for recreation to Pennsylvania's picturesque rural communities. The decorated barns were a popular attraction, as they were easily visible from public roadways winding through the hills of Berks and Lehigh counties along the old Route 22 corridor. For the first time, these unique artistic expressions were subject to the curiosity of visitors eager for colorful explanations of the rich and distinctive cultural landscape of the region.

In these early decades, the artist Milton Hill witnessed the development of outside interest in the barn stars, and, later, even benefited from the increased exposure to new tourist markets. However, this benefit came with the heavy price of cultural misrepresentation.

In the absence of any widely disseminated information on the subject, authors and entrepreneurs hurried to fill the void with travel journalism that was often fraught with rampant commercialism, fabrications, and dubious interpretations of the culture. Many misconceptions about decorated barns originated during this time, and have been perpetuated into the present day.

This includes the fictional narrative of the "hex sign," a term that was coined in the 1920s by journalists from outside the area who promoted Pennsylvania as a tourist destination. By virtue of national distribution, these unsubstantiated and culturally inaccurate accounts by alleged "experts" rapidly reached their eager audiences, who became enchanted with the notion of the "hex sign" as a cultural icon. As a result of this case of widespread and pervasive misinformation, even locals today remain divided on the issue.

In 1924, a retired Congregational minister, antiquarian, photographer, and author of romanticized travelogues, Rev. Wallace Nutting (1861 - 1941) of Framingham, Massachusetts, released the first detailed account from a traveler's eyes of southeastern Pennsylvania's decorated barns to national audiences in his book *Pennsylvania Beautiful*.

The reverend's very brief summary of the barns, nearly hidden amidst his

A pen and ink drawing from Wallace Nutting's *Pennsylvania Beautiful* in 1924, showing a split "Dutch" door, with a decorated door hood. Wallace Nutting mistakenly compounded stories of protection from the supernatural with these door hoods, and paved the way for the popularity of the term "hex sign."

A pen and ink drawing of a barn in Earl Township, Berks County, included in Wallace Nutting's *Pennsylvania Beautiful*. The drawing was originally accompanied by the caption "A Witch-Foot Barn," alleging the false notion that the decorations were emblems used to keep witches away from the barn.

romantic photographs of bucolic landscapes and line drawings of colonial antiques, was singlehandedly responsible for inspiring the misconception that the region's barn star decorations were supernatural in origin.[1] Nutting wrote:

> "They are a decoration sometimes applied on the door heads or on or about the door. They are supposed to be a continuance of a very ancient tradition, according to which these decorative marks were potent to protect the barn, or more particularly the cattle, from the influence of witches. It is understood by those who are acquainted with witches that those ladies are particularly likely to harm cattle. As the wealth of the farmer was in his stock, contained in his remarkably substantial barn, the hexafoos was added to its decoration as a kind of spiritual or demoniac lightning-rod!"[2]

Although Nutting never actually used the word "hex sign," his phonetic spelling of the obscure Pennsylvania Dutch term "*Hexefuss*," a term translating to "witch's foot," was the direct inspiration for "hex sign" in predominant use today.[3]

Was there any truth to Nutting's claims? Who would be better to offer their appraisal of this notion than Milton Hill himself, a third generation painter of the stars in the heart of Berks County in the epicenter of the artistic tradition?

Milton Hill had already been painting barn stars for well over twenty years by the time that Wallace Nutting's accounts of Pennsylvania barns were first published. As a Pennsylvania Dutchman, he was also no stranger to stories and folklore associated with witchcraft and the supernatural. In most rural communities in the region, it was indeed once common place in previous generations to attribute misfortune, illness, and calamity to supernatural forces, and such stories abounded in Berks County.[4]

Milton Hill's resistance to the use of the word "hex sign" was actually rooted in his awareness of the serious implication of the word. In Pennsylvania Dutch, the word *Hex* holds a dual significance, referring to both any willful curse or grudge placed by one individual upon another, and refers as well as

"A Decorated Barn, Lehigh County" by Wallace Nutting, showing an unusual arrangement of sunbursts, arches, moons, and other decorations. *Pennsylvania Beautiful, 1924.*

to the individual responsible for the curse—i.e., one who practices witchcraft, a sorcerer.[5] Suspicions of witchcraft were traditionally and anecdotally associated with common place scenarios on the farm, such as when butter would not form in the churn, or when livestock behaved strangely.

This was precisely the case with "Witchcraft Road," which bordered the Hill Farm directly to the north. Although this rural road in Windsor Township officially received its name in the 1970s, many generations of residents referred to the ridge where the road wound as *Hexebarrich,* or Witchcraft Hill.[6] Allegedly, farmers transporting livestock along the base of this ridge claimed that the cattle would spook, stand stock-still, and could not be persuaded to move forward. This unusual and inconvenient animal behavior gave rise to the name of the road. Whether or not most people in the area actually believed that any witchcraft was at work, the name of the road records the old narratives associated with the neighborhood.

Milton would also have been familiar with the common knowledge of formerly widespread cultural practices used to protect *against* witchcraft in rural communities throughout the region. These traditional practices—such as placing a broom by the entrance of the home, nailing a horseshoe above the stable door, sprinkling salt on the windowsill, carrying the resin of the herb asafetida in a bundle around one's neck or nailing a bundle in the cow stalls—were once widely practiced or at least well known in Berks County. While such ritual beliefs were once prevalent, and common people integrated such ideas into their daily lives for generations, other more specialized practices were reserved for elders in the community who were respected (and in some cases feared) for their ability to counteract the supernatural, heal illness, and bless humans, livestock, and land.

Collectively, these practices were known as *Braucherei,* a Pennsylvania Dutch word for ritual customs, but the word "powwowing" was also widely used among speakers of English.[7] Although a practitioner (*Braucher* or powwower) could be found in most communities throughout the region, many rituals associated with daily life were commonly practiced at home and on the farm by anyone with enough knowledge of the old traditions.

Milton's mother Ellen Elizabeth (Wanner) Hill was particularly knowledgeable in this area and was known to have engaged in certain old customs on the Hill family farm. Her granddaughter and namesake,

Ellen Elizabeth (Hill) Heffner, recalled seeing her grandmother rise at dawn and uproot Canadian thistles before the buds went to flower, and gather them into a burlap bag. A blessing was uttered quietly as the bag, thistles and all, was taken to the butcher house and incinerated to ashes in the butchering cauldron and then scattered on the land—presumably to ritually expel the thistles from the property. Although Ellen witnessed her grandmother perform this old ritual, she never asked her for any clarification, because such things were not always openly explained, for fear that the process would not be entirely effective.[8]

Grandmother Ellen had also employed remedies and cures including a classic treatment for earache in children, whereby first she irrigated the ear canal with smoke from her tobacco. Then she asked the child to urinate in a clean container, and the warm urine was used to flush the ear canal. As urine is generally sterile and harmless, this old remedy, combined with a specific prayer, was widely practiced throughout Berks and Lehigh with positive results.[9]

Milton Hill and his family would have been well aware of both the benefits as well as the occasional controversy[10] surrounding powwowing and the ritual traditions of the region. At the same time he was also knowledgeable and experienced enough to know that his artwork and the traditional barn stars of the region were not at all part of a powwower's repertoire, who instead preferred the creation of written blessings which were concealed within the architecture of the barn.[11] Barn stars were reserved for professional painters, and not for the ritual removal or prevention of a hex.

Nevertheless, the not-so-subtle irony of Witchcraft Road's proximity to the home of one of the leading painters of so-called "hex signs" was probably not lost on Milton, who deeply resented that his work was mistakenly linked to tales of the supernatural. The story of the road at *Hexebarrich*, despite its location, had nothing at all to do with Milton's work, or the work of the generations of painters before him throughout the community. When a group of visitors from outside of the region would stop by the Hill farm to take pictures, Milton Hill would correct any of their mistaken associations with a gentle reminder that his stars "were just for nice," and "never for [a] hex."[12]

Although Rev. Wallace Nutting's accounts of the decorated barns had mistakenly associated the region's brightly colored barn stars with tales of witchcraft, it is interesting to note that Nutting had described his subject in an unusual way—as "marks" "on or about the door"—rather than with precise descriptions of painted stars in elaborate arrangements on the siding of the barns.[13] Despite Nutting's obvious errors, there is a kernel of truth to his account.

Nutting was not the only person to investigate the perception that farmers would occasionally carve or draw something called a "*Hexefuss*" (plural "*Hexefiess*") in chalk on a door, if they feared the influence of the

Barn stars were not originally intended for supernatural protection. Instead, local barn owners concealed written blessings, such as this early example, written as a protective inscription for the years 1827 to 1831, invoking the Holy Trinity as well as the stars and planets. *Courtesy of the Philip and Muriel Berman Museum of Art at Ursinus College.*

supernatural. Nutting's description follows precisely what fellow Harvard graduate, archaeologist, and collector of early American material culture Henry Chapman Mercer (1856-1930) documented in his field notes ca. 1900 in his explorations of the border region between Berks and Lehigh counties.[14]

Mercer's detailed notes confirm, however, that he was not describing the barn star tradition, but rather a subtle form of apotropaic ritual markings written in chalk on the interiors of barn doors far from the public eye. Although it is uncertain if Mercer himself was the source of Nutting's accounts, both of these men were part of the upper echelon of the avocational collectors of early Americana, and were well aware of one another's work.[15]

Coincidentally, Mercer was curator of the archaeological collections at the University of Pennsylvania Museum, and his interest in the *Hexefuss* coincided with that of Penn faculty member and folklorist, Dr. Edwin Miller Fogel, who also documented the idea of the "*Hexefuss*" in his field work at the turn of the twentieth century as a chalk marking used by farmers to ward off the influence of the supernatural.[16]

A powwower's astrological barn blessing discovered near Kutztown. The blessing was written on a red card, wrapped in a sheet of lead, and hidden under the floor boards of the barn at the time of its construction in the 1840s. *Private Collection.*

This was an ancient ritual marking that resembled the actual foot of an animal, such as the five-toed hind foot of a frog, or the upright foot of a goose. In some rare instances farmers would even nail the actual foot of a goose onto a barn door for protection from evil.[17] This ritual, however, bore no visual similarity with the colorful painted stars on the barns, and Mercer and Fogel would likely have been aware of Nutting's error. Interestingly enough, neither Fogel nor Mercer ever managed to photograph a single supposed instance of a ritually applied *Hexefuss* on a barn door. Perhaps this was because they never actually saw one with their own eyes?

What is abundantly clear, however, is that Nutting, Fogel, and Mercer were citing an altogether separate practice from the painting of barn stars. The conflation of these ideas, however, ushered in an era when such colorful misconceptions were welcomed by both popular audiences and the self-taught gentlemen-scholars of the times.

In the decades that followed, the release of Nutting's book, the story took on a life of its own and gradually evolved into the full-blown myth of the "hex sign." The new hybrid term, combining the Pennsylvania Dutch word for "witch" and the English word "sign" was easier to manage than Nutting's use of *Hexefuss*. Journalists preferred this simplification, which was later embraced by the region's tourist boom during the 1940s and 50s.[18]

The widespread popular use of the word "hex sign" eventually extended into other forms of American culture by the mid-1940s, including the jargon of advertisements, but most especially professional sporting events. Some athletic competitors would "put the hex sign"[19] on their opponents with a gesture involving the connection of the thumb and forefinger that appeared in newspapers and on television as a bad omen for the other team, and used to "jinx" the outcome of the game.

With the conflation of this kind of widespread pop-culture reference with Pennsylvania Dutch folk culture, it is small wonder that barn star painters like Milton Hill were defensive about their work. Several public statements that Milton made to journalists in the 1950s show his concern about being misidentified as a creator of "hexes," as he well-

MAGIC AND FOLK MEDICINE
See a water dowser in action and learn about the many different kinds of divining rods. Learn the meaning of the various hex sign patterns; watch a hex sign painter plying his trade.

Despite the best of intentions, even the Pennsylvania Folklife Society's second annual Harvest Frolic promotional materials included insinuations that something magical was involved in the creation of Milton's work, and perpetuated false stereotypes of the art form. *Pennsylvania German Cultural Heritage Center, Kutztown University.*

visitors thought that Milton was deliberately concealing the truth about his work. His adamant responses to the contrary seemed to provoke the incredulity of tourists who perceived that a hidden undercurrent of occult activity was pervasive within the local culture. Others simply dismissed Milton, suggesting that perhaps he was ignorant of the "true" origins of the artistic tradition. While not necessarily common among all tourists, these kinds of attitudes were an indicator that some outsiders visited the region because of the perception that the culture was "frozen in time" or a curious anachronism in a modern age. Fueled by stereotypes of the "Dumb Dutchman," the result was a class of privileged tourists who presumed that they knew much more about the folk culture than the Pennsylvania Dutch people themselves.

Coupled with a steadily growing interest among tourists with the Plain Communities of the Amish and Old Order Mennonites, false associations between these religious groups and the decorated barns added yet another layer of misconception to the equation. Under the false impression that all Pennsylvania Dutch were Amish, tourists associated a wide range of unrelated features of the culture with the Plain Communities, and this became firmly established in the 1950s with the rise of Lancaster County as a regional tourist destination.

Despite the fact that the Plain Communities tended to avoid exterior decorations on their homes and farms in keeping with their religious commitment to plain living, visitors to Lancaster County today will likely see commercial hex sign plaques

understood the implications of such a word. Much to Milton's and his family's dismay, a photograph of the artist even appeared in the *New York Times* above the caption "Devilish Design."[20] Such associations with evil, even when considered tongue-in-cheek humor, understandably did not sit well with him.

Oddly enough, by the time that Milton began to interact more regularly with visitors to the region, the idea of the "hex sign" was so firmly embedded in the tourist literature that for sale at tourist gift shops and applied to storefronts, restaurants, travel agencies, and commercial attractions all along the Route 30 corridor, marketed as original features of the "Amish Country."

This is in part due to regional tourist publications throughout southeastern and central Pennsylvania which suggested that the barn stars originated with Amish artists, when in actuality these designs were never found on barns within the Plain Communities in Lancaster. In fact, with the exception of the northern border with Berks and Lebanon, the barn stars are largely absent from Lancaster County, because the Amish and Old Order Mennonites typically do not decorate their barns, and these Plain Communities account for a large portion of the agricultural properties throughout the county. This is not necessarily a rule across all Anabaptist groups, but only rarely in certain Mennonite communities have some farmers within the past generation or so, painted their barns with stars. Only a few examples of this can be found in the vicinity of Kutztown, where some Mennonite property owners have restored their farms to their original states, including the stars that adorned the barns.[21] The Mennonites in the Kutztown area were not the original owners of these properties, but instead are descended from Lancaster County families that purchased large tracts of land in Berks in the 1950s and 1960s, and today are the keepers of some of the county's most picturesque open spaces in the East Penn Valley.

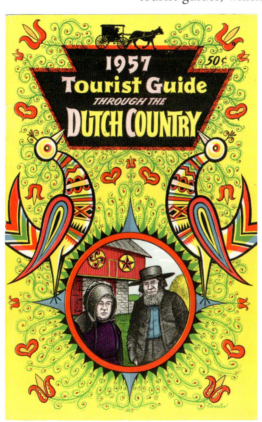

Tourist Guide by the Pennsylvania Dutch Folklore Center, Franklin and Marshall College, later known as the Pennsylvania Folklife Society. Some of the illustrated covers perpetuated the misconception that the Amish painted barn stars. *Pennsylvania German Cultural Heritage Center, Kutztown University.*

The Kutztown Folk Festival, founded in 1950 by the Pennsylvania Dutch Folklore Center at Franklin and Marshall College (later called the Pennsylvania Folklife Society), served to energize the tourist industry by promoting, not only the largest folk-cultural festival of its kind in the nation, but also some of the first illustrated tourism guides to the region. The trio of scholars who founded the festival, Dr. Alfred Shoemaker, Dr. J. William Frey, and Dr. Don Yoder, also created the first of these early tourist guides, which featured scholarly photo essays on different aspects of the folk culture. Unfortunately, a series of lavishly illustrated covers for these annual tourist guides perpetuated the misconception that the Amish painted barn stars. Dr. Don Yoder lamented this oversight by the Society's editorial staff, who understood only too late the impact of such publications seemingly sanctioned by the Society.[22]

Nevertheless, the Society's positive impact on the Pennsylvania Dutch community was far-reaching, especially through the highly successful efforts of the Kutztown Folk Festival. In showcasing the local bearers of folk traditions to national public audiences, the Festival celebrated and revitalized the region's distinctive arts, customs, trades and language. It was at the Festival that Milton Hill's artistry blossomed into an altogether more colorful and sophisticated iteration, and his work became legendary.

Milton Hill painting at his display booth at the Kutztown Folk Festival in the Folk Art Building sometime in the 1960s. During this time, his artwork blossomed into a diverse range of designs and patterns beyond his classic, signature Hill Star. Many examples of these new developments appear in Milton's colorful display on the wall behind his painting demonstration table. *Courtesy of Lee S. Heffner & Family.*

CHAPTER V

The Tradition Evolves

In 1950, the culture of the Pennsylvania Dutch was forever changed by the establishment of the Kutztown Pennsylvania Dutch Folk Festival—the first festival of its kind to showcase the traditions, language, music, foodways, and arts of an American regional folk culture. Founded by Alfred L. Shoemaker, J. William Frey, and Don Yoder of the Pennsylvania Folklife Society, the festival was a community event that combined both the public and the academic realms into a celebration that inspired scores of regional festivals nationwide.[1]

The Festival introduced the concept of *folklife* into American parlance, defined as the sum total of a culture's traditions, including agriculture, the arts, trades, and day-to-day domestic life.[2] The Festival staff actively sought bearers of tradition in a wide variety of fields, with the hopes that the festival would become an important venue to simultaneously document, preserve, and demonstrate these traditions for the public.

The Festival's executive director, Dr. Alfred L. Shoemaker, and the Society's secretary, Olive G. Zehner, recognized the importance of Milton Hill's work as the preeminent barn star painter in the region, and were excited to engage with him as part of the festival programming.[3]

An interesting, yet highly fictionalized story of Milton Hill has been circulated over the years, suggesting that he was the co-inventor of the first commercial barn star painted on sign board at the suggestion of Dr. Shoemaker at the first folk festival in 1950.[4] The truth of the matter is that the specifics of the story have been embellished over time by generations of festival-goers, and much of the story is contradicted by documents and family accounts from the period.

The story claims that visitors at the first Festival in 1950 saw Milton painting barn stars on large wooden panels set up like a barn on the festival grounds. Fascinated by his

Above: A classic Milton Hill Star, painted on commercial masonite signboard sometime in the late 1950s or early 1960s. This technical development in painting surface revolutionized the art of Pennsylvania's barn stars, allowing the stars to be applied to any type of building and at any location throughout the world. Courtesy of Phares W. & Mabel M. (Heffner) Fry (granddaughter of Milton & Gertrude Hill) & Family.

Above: A spread of folklife activities advertising the work of Milton Hill among the highlights of the 10th annual Pennsylvania Dutch Folk Festival in 1959. *Pennsylvania German Cultural Heritage Center, Kutztown University.*

Below: Milton Hill, painting at the Kutztown Folk Festival, while founding executive director Festival, Dr. Alfred Shoemaker, promotes Milton's display. *Courtesy of Lee S. Heffner & Family.*

work, the visitors inquired with him about where they could purchase his art, and Milton informed them that unfortunately he only painted on barns. This was not particularly helpful to visitors from New York, New Jersey, or California, who had neither barns, nor geographic proximity to Berks County. Dr. Alfred Shoemaker then allegedly had the idea to hire a carpenter to cut large circles out of plywood for Milton to paint on. Some stories even claim that this new development took place "over night," alleging that Milton stayed up that very first evening to prepare several stars which he promptly sold the following day. From thence forth, according to the story, Milton was able to paint and sell his work directly to visitors in a completely new format that had never been previously explored.

While accounts of this ilk have been repeated many times since Milton's first appearance at the festival, the actual chronology of the events is much more complicated and uncertain.

Beginning sometime in the year 1949, Shoemaker and Zehner visited him with the intention of securing Milton's commitment to demonstrate at the festival on its inaugural year in the summer of 1950. Unfortunately, due to the high demand for his painting work during the summer months, Milton was unable to participate in the festival during his busiest season. He regretfully declined the invitation to attend, but said that he might consider it in the future.[5]

As a compromise, the Festival staff requested samples of his work to display in his absence, but this was also impossible because up until this point Milton only painted his stars directly on the wooden siding of local barns. Instead, the Festival encouraged visitors to see the countryside for themselves, and included many images of local decorated barns in the 1950 Festival Program.[6]

By the following year in 1951, visitors were so eager to see the decorated barns for themselves, that the Festival took busloads of visitors through the countryside to see the work of Hill and other artists, as a way to explore the open-air gallery of local folk art in the hills just outside of Kutztown. Descriptions of the tour, which extended from Kutztown through Lenhartsville and over the Blue Mountain above Hamburg, emphasized "the huge elaborate circular designs of many colors"—a nod to the presence of Milton's work in that region.[7]

It was during this time that Milton would have had his first encounters with visitors to the Festival, who may have inquired about the availability of his work. We may never know exactly how the story unfolded, and whether Dr. Shoemaker ever truly had a role in suggesting that Milton first paint on

Above Left: An original Milton Hill Star from the early years of the Festival. *Courtesy of Gwenn Davis.*
Right: Milton's VIP Passes to the Kutztown Folk Festival and Harvest Frolic. *Courtesy of Lee S. Heffner & Family.*

Milton J. Hill demonstrates barn star painting on the forebay of a barn display at the Kutztown Folk Festival in 1955. *Courtesy of Jason Graver.*

Above: Milton Hill's booth at the Kutztown Folk Festival in July of 1959 featured a wide variety of new designs as well as his signature star patterns. While old black and white photographs from this era did not capture the colorful effects of his work, it is easy to see how Milton's designs had changed with the incorporation of new techniques and painting surfaces. *Courtesy of Lee S. Heffner & Family.*

Below: A Milton Hill Star with a monochromatic border, a concept with which Milton often experimented over the years to produce a variety of subtle patterns. *Courtesy of Lee S. Heffner & Family.*

commercial signboard. If Shoemaker was responsible for this, he never mentioned it in any of his detailed accounts of the early highlights of the festival.

Nevertheless, by 1953, when Milton appeared for the first time at the fourth annual Festival as a demonstrator,[8] he had already embraced the idea of painting his stars on Masonite, a new commercial composite signboard. Milton scribed each and every one of his stars on signboard, just like his stars painted on barn siding, giving them an authentic feel, despite the novelty of the signboard surface.

In addition to Milton's display of hand-painted stars on commercial signboard, Milton did ascend a ladder and paint on a large demonstration area made to look like the forebay of a barn at the Festival. The set was complete with a fenced-in barn yard, where some wandering livestock added to the rural feel of the festival grounds. Among the scant photographs documenting this live demonstration are ones showing him painting a large 8-pointed star in 1955. It is possible that Milton may have participated in this painting demonstration over several years—perhaps even since his earliest appearance at the festival in 1953.

That very same year that Milton first attended the festival as a folklife demonstrator and craftsman, artist John J. "Johnny" Ott of Lenhartsville (1890-1964) also arrived at the Kutztown Folk Festival for the very first time,[82] and both artists offered competing explanations for the origins of the art form. While Milton Hill maintained that his work was an extension of an old tradition of painting stars on barns, Johnny Ott assumed the title of "Professor of Hexology," and explained that his work was imbued with magical power. He told tourists that each design not only had a succinct meaning, but also served as a charm for a wide variety of concerns and infirmities—everything from assurance of success and prosperity, to assistance with love and romance. These new concocted commercial meanings ensured that Ott's customers not only received a piece of his work, but also a story—a tall-tale that created lasting memorable encounters with the exotic "Hexologist" of the Dutch Country.[9]

Milton was no showman like Johnny Ott, but his work was able to proverbially stand up on its own. After a career of over fifty years painting barns, Milton's work showed a level of sophistication and refinement that rapidly earned him recognition as one of the most celebrated artists of the festival. Images of Milton Hill appeared in national newspapers like the *New York Times*.[10] By the opening day of the festival the following year in 1954, Milton and Dr. Shoemaker were featured on NBC primetime television on the show "Home" with an interview by Arlene Francis, airing across the nation. This and other national media appearances highlighted Milton as not only the foremost painter at the Festival, but also of the entire culture of Pennsylvania Dutch.

Despite the artist's newfound celebrity status, Milton Hill remained a humble and introspective person who avoided the limelight whenever possible. Nevertheless, the increased demand for his work and the adoption of new techniques on commercial signboard, allowed him to experiment with a wider range of complex patterns and diversified color palettes.

Although he was more accustomed to painting on the rough texture of weathered barn

Above: A variety of classic and adapted Milton Hill star patterns from the Kutztown Folk Festival. *Courtesy of Dorian (Derr) Fetherolf, top; and Phares W. & Mabel M. (Heffner) Fry, bottom three.*

Above: Festival photograph of Milton and his sister-in-law, Sallie Hoffa, against a stunning display of his work. *Courtesy of the Pennsylvania Folklife Society Archive, Myrin Library, Ursinus College.*

Below: An original star by Milton Hill, painted ca. 1960 on commercial Masonite sign board. This particular star includes the use of metallic gold paint, which was unusual for Milton's work. *Courtesy of Eric Claypoole.*

siding, he quickly adapted to his newly preferred painting medium—pressed masonite disks, which he meticulously cut out by hand with a coping saw. Milton continued to neatly scribe each of his designs into the surface of his sign board just like he did on barn siding, and these clean edges served to accurately guide his brush across the smooth surface.

Milton began to experiment with color theory, especially with subtle alterations of color in his signature star bursts, which had increased in complexity from his standard eight points to as many as thirty-two. On some of these new patterns, he began with a deep goldenrod yellow on the outermost star points, and lightened the color for each successive layer of points, gradually progressing to a very pale yellow in the center. This glowing color gradient produced a sense of depth as well as the optical illusion of pulsation and expansion from the center of the design. These types of sophisticated techniques set Milton's work apart from other artists of the era, such as

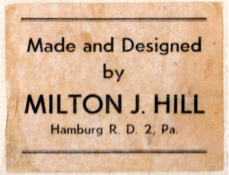

Top: Milton Hill used this tin stencil to mark the back of his barn stars on sign board with black spray paint. *Pennsylvania German Cultural Heritage Center, Kutztown University, Gift of Esther (Hill) & Harold Derr & Family.*
Left: An early paper label, presumably predating Milton's stenciled signature on barn star disks. *Courtesy of Ivan. E. Hoyt & Family.* **Right:** Milton's stenciled signature. *Courtesy of Dorian (Derr) Fetherolf.*

Johnny Ott, whose designs tended to be flat compilations of stylized visual elements such as stars, hearts, birds, tulips, human figures and other motifs.

Perhaps because Milton's original barn stars were typically painted in solid colors on rough wooden siding, he began to experiment with adding surface texture. This created a sense of visual interest on the smooth signboard, and enhanced the hand-painted effect. Recalling his days as a grain painter, Milton was able to produce a marbleized effect with nothing more than a rag, a dry brush, a piece of newspaper, or even his finger. While most of his designs featured a slight gradient in the very center point by selectively removing the paint, he extended this technique into his borders, for a mottled effect. This combination of precise geometric forms with irregular applications of paint produced an organic appearance that suggested the blossoming of flowers and other biological forms.

Another new development for Milton Hill was that after fifty years of painting, he finally began to sign his work. For this purpose, printed labels were affixed to some of these earliest pieces. Although his penmanship was impeccable and he certainly could have painted his signature, he preferred instead to stencil his name and mailing address on the reverse of each of his stars with the inscription: "Made & Designed by Milton J. Hill Hamburg, R.D. 2 PA." This ensured that his work could be easily identified, and additional signs

Demonstrating at the Kutztown Folk Festival in the 1960s, Milton Hill teaches children visiting the Festival the finer points of his art. *Courtesy of the Pennsylvania Folklife Society Archive, Myrin Library, Ursinus College.*

could be ordered by writing to the address provided on the back of the star.

Milton created an impressive display of his stars at the festival by engineering a series of lateral racks along the wall of the Festival's Folk Art Building. He transformed the space by introducing the old kitchen table and patterned table cloth which he used for painting at home in his studio in the old henhouse, as well as a variety of chairs including his old rocker. This created a welcoming space where visitors and friends could stop by to watch the master at work, and provided enough informal seating for his grandchildren and great-grandchildren to visit him throughout the festival week.

Well dressed for the occasion, Milton was meticulous about his public appearance, and wouldn't dare to show up at the festival without wearing a dress-shirt and tie under his painters overalls. He generally alternated between a stylish fedora and his flat-top professional painters cap, depending on his preference and what the situation called for.

Visitors would find him leaning forward over his painting, with his gaze focused on his brush. The strap from his painter's overalls would often hang over his right arm as he worked, due to a benign fatty tumor on his shoulder that prevented the strap from staying in place. Milton was quiet while he worked, and was sparing with stories and explanations. Milton preferred that his work would speak for itself, and his sales were by no means diminished by his demeanor. Instead, visitors were drawn to his work, and more inclined to stay for a moment to watch him work the brush. Children were especially mesmerized by his steady hand.

The Festival was truly in its hey-day by 1960, and Dr. Alfred L. Shoemaker and the Pennsylvania Folklife Society ambitiously endeavored to create a new folklife museum and satellite festival grounds along the Lincoln Highway just outside of Lancaster.[12] At great expense, the Society constructed a brand new decorated brick-end barn to serve as the headquarters and archive.[13] In 1961 the Society held their first autumn event, the Pennsylvania Dutch Harvest Frolic, where visitors could watch the barn construction in process. Milton Hill was one of two artists to decorate the barns on the site,[14] including a smaller barn that was eventually used as a theater to show a documentary on the Amish. This new venue in Lancaster was short-lived, however, because the Society ran into financial troubles, despite the fact that the Kutztown Folk Festival continued to flourish as a successful folklife celebration.[15]

Above: Barn decorating demonstrations for the Pennsylvania Folklife Society's Lancaster County museum site, including Milton J. Hill (right) and another unidentified artist (left). **Below:** Milton Hill's painting demonstration by the brick barn at the 1961 Harvest Frolic. Photos by Vincent R. Tortora, photographer for the Pennsylvania Folklife Society and proprietor of Photo Arts Press, Manheim, Pennsylvania.

In the early 60s, two of Milton's dear granddaughters, Dorian, daughter of Harold J. and Esther L. (Hill) Derr, and Carol, daughter of Milton D. and June R. (Schappell) Hill, used to ride with him each day to the festival.[16] Dorian recalls watching over her grandfather's shoulder while he painted, until one day a woman visiting from outside the area scolded her for being a distraction. "Young lady, you are standing too close to that man while he is painting!" Milton looked up from his work only long enough to smile and inform the visitor "That's my granddaughter." Dorian and Carol remained close by his side throughout the early days of the festival, and recall Milton's most successful day of sales in the early 60s. On that day, he made several hundred dollars, which was a lot of money back then. Milton was ecstatic, and eager to share his success with his wife Gertrude. Headed for home with a pocket full of money and a fat cigar in his mouth, Milton loaded Dorian and Carol into the family's *Maschien*—a black 1950 Buick Special, with a state of the art Straight 8 Fireball engine and Dynaflow transmission. Despite its description, this hulking gas-guzzler featured a characteristically slow acceleration that was also perfectly suited to Milton's most unhurried driving style. However, on that most auspicious of days, Dorian and Carol could sense their grampy's excitement, as the car sped down the old Kutztown Road faster than they'd ever seen him drive. Upon glancing at the speedometer, the girls saw that grampy was driving a whopping 40 miles per hour—a new all time record for Milton Hill!

Although these later years at the festival were among Milton's happiest and most successful, they are also remembered for a terrible tragedy the family suffered in 1963. Milton and Gertrude's oldest son John L. Hill, was fatally injured in an accident around dinner time on Tuesday July 2, when his freshly painted red work-truck was struck by his nephew Robert Hill's car along the Virginville Road. John was turning into a driveway at the top of a hill at a blind curve, and Robert did not see his uncle's truck until it was too late. While Robert suffered no significant injuries, his Uncle John sustained severe trauma to the head, and was in a coma for 8 days

Above: Four Milton Hill designs documented in 1960s Kutztown Folk Festival photographs, recreated by Sarah E. Edris of Mohrsville at the Pennsylvania German Cultural Heritage Center at Kutztown University.

Milton J. Hill in his painting studio in the old hen house at the Hill family farm. An example of Milton's marbled technique is visible behind the artist on the green border of an eight-pointed star. An ornate woodstove stands in the foreground, and in the background, a portrait of his mother Ellen E. (Wanner) Hill hangs on the wall. *Original black and white photograph courtesy of the Pennsylvania Folklife Society Archive, Myrin Library, Ursinus College. New digital rendering in color by the Pennsylvania German Cultural Heritage Center, Kutztown University.*

before passing away on the evening of July 10.[17] John's wife Melva was left a widow, and their two sons and two daughters lost their father. This was a particularly difficult time for the family, and Milton and Gertrude were devastated by the loss of their oldest son, whom Milton called "the artist of the family."

This tragedy was felt on many levels, as Milton had also considered John the inheritor of his artistic legacy, and lamented that his son would not be able to continue the family tradition. Up until the time of his passing, John was best known for the painting of livestock murals on local barns, and he had even continued to paint his father's Hill Star designs after Milton retired from ascending the high ladders sometime in the late 1950s.

It was John, in fact, who had repainted his father's stars on the barn at the Hill Farm sometime around 1960, by which time Milton had already fully retired from painting on barns and was over the age of seventy.

By this time, Milton's art had become increasingly tied to his studio work. He had converted an old hen house into his studio, and outfitted it with an old kitchen table as a painting surface and an ornate potbellied stove for heat. The studio gave him enough room to paint, to store his supplies, and still have space for an old rocker to sit and rest when he needed it. A full wall of window sashes on one side of the hen house provided Milton with enough natural light for his painting.

Above: Ethel Smith of Hamburg and Milton Hill by the barnyard fence on the Hill family farm. Milton's stars in the background appear to be different than in other images of the barn from the same period. It is possible that the stars were in the process of being repainted by Milton and Gertrude's oldest son John L. Hill at the time that the photo was shot, ca. 1960. *Courtesy of Beth Humma & Shire Valley Legacies.*

Below: Milton's business sign, painted and hand-lettered by Ethel Smith, which hung on the corn crib at the Hill family farm along the Virginville Road. *Courtesy of Lee S. Heffner & Family.*

Milton used a second chicken house on the property as his woodshop, where he stored his masonite sheets, and cut out his circular disks meticulously by hand with a coping saw. He would carry the disks to his studio, where he would clamp them to his table for layout with the use of his *Zaerkel* (a pair of compass dividers). This step first of clamping the disk down to his painting surface was especially important for many of his new designs, which often required some geometric points of reference outside of the circumference of the disk surface. He used a protective sheet under his disk where he could anchor one point of the compass in order to scribe arcs onto the outermost edges of the border. While Milton much preferred painting on the rough surface of old barn wood, he understood the advantages of his new format and used them to the fullest extent.

As Milton invented new patterns, he would invite friends and family to join him in the studio for some constructive criticism

Above: Milton's open air art gallery along the snow fence by his hen house studio, taken as a publicity photograph for the Pennsylvania Folklife Society by Vincent R. Tortora. *Courtesy of Lee S. Heffner & Family.*

Below: A Milton Hill Star on display at the Pennsylvania Dutch Gift-Haus at Roadside America, a popular destination for regional tourism. *Photography by Lee S. Heffner.*

and suggestions. Lee Heffner recalls being summoned frequently by his grandfather who excitedly bid him to "*Kumm mol mit mir zum Schapp*" (Come with me to the shed). Milton would then unveil his most recent creations and ask for advice: "*Denkscht's verkaaft?*" (Do you think it will sell?). When asked where and how he came up with his newest patterns, Milton would simply point to his head and smile, as he never used paper to plan his work in advance.

Milton's studio painting eventually became his mainstay, not just for creating stock to sell at the Festival, but throughout the year. He eventually had a large hand-lettered sign attached to the corncrib by the road which read: "Milton J. Hill, Creator of Authentic Barn Symbols." The sign was made by his friend from the Festival, Ethel Smith of Hamburg, who insisted that he properly market his work to the public with a professional sign. While Milton was not particularly fond

of the wording, and did not agree with the idea with the notion that his stars were "symbolic," he truly appreciated Ethel's tribute to his work, and kept the sign hanging by the Virginville Road throughout the entirety of his late career.

When the staff from the Kutztown Folk Festival or photographers from the press came to the farm to visit Milton's studio, he would line up his stars along a section of old wooden snow fence in the yard, as an open-air gallery where his work could be admired and photographed in full sunlight.

In a rare piece of family footage, recorded around 1960 by his son-in-law Harold J. Derr on Super-8 film, Milton arranges his finest examples of his 4' and 3' stars along the garden fence across the yard from this studio. It is clear from this early family videography that Milton was truly in his prime as an artist and in the most productive phase of his long career. Dressed in his painter's overalls and cap, with a slate-gray work shirt, Milton walks each piece out the door of his hen house studio, across the lawn, and arranges the stars in sequence, and then one by one walks each piece back into the studio. This iconic formation along the snow fence was created again and again for visitors, customers, friends, and family, as an unassuming display of the ever-evolving fruits of Milton's creative genius.

Although visitors from out of town frequented the Hill farm to acquire Milton's work, by far his most prestigious visit came in mid-October of 1964, on behalf of the staff of Democratic Vice-Presidential Candidate Hubert H. Humphrey. Although Milton did not meet the candidate

Above Left: Selected stills from footage of Milton J. Hill placing his work along the edge of the garden fence, taken by his son-in-law Harold J. Derr, ca. 1960 on Super-8 film. *Courtesy of Dorian (Derr) Fetherolf & Family.*
Right: A Milton Hill star. *Courtesy of the Freyberger Family.*

Above: A Milton Hill rosette star was prominently featured as a statement of cultural solidarity in the campaign visit of then Democratic Vice-Presidential Candidate Hubert H. Humphrey at Penn Square in Reading City on October 15, 1964. *Pennsylvania German Cultural Heritage Center, Kutztown University of Pennsylvania.*

Below: A rosette star identical to the one presented to Hubert Humphrey. *Courtesy of Lee S. Heffner & Family.*

in person, Mr. Humphrey made a public appearance at Penn Square in Reading City on October 15, where he held aloft an original star by Milton Hill to show his support and solidarity with the rural Pennsylvania Dutch. Humphrey and the Presidential Candidate Lyndon B. Johnson later secured the victory in the November election, making Humphrey the 38th Vice President of the United States. Whatever became of his Milton Hill barn star is unknown, but the photographs of Mr. Humphrey showing solidarity with the Pennsylvania Dutch resonated with the people of Berks County that their local culture would receive such notable attention on a national level during a presidential campaign.

Although Milton Hill's appearance yet again in the national spotlight was only momentary, his most long-lasting publicity came in the form of a series of photographs shot by professional photographer Vincent R. Tortora (1927-2003) at the Kutztown Folk Festival. Tortora, who operated a photographic publishing company from his home in Manheim, Lancaster County, specialized

An unattributed publicity photograph taken at the Kutztown Folk Festival for the Pennsylvania Folklife Society, likely taken by prolific photographer Vincent R. Tortora of Photo Arts Press, Manheim, PA. Tortora was best known for his photography and his 1959 award-winning documentary film "The Old Order Amish."
Courtesy of the Pennsylvania Folklife Society Archive, Myrin Library, Ursinus College.

Above: Postcard of Milton posing for the camera at the Kutztown Folk Festival, ca. 1965. *Heilman Collection.*
Below: One of Milton's flashy new patterns pioneered on commercial sign board at the Kutztown Folk Festival. Recreated by the Pennsylvania German Cultural Heritage Center Staff, Kutztown University.

in documenting the Old Order Amish community in colorful tourist booklets, as well as black and white photo essays which for the *Pennsylvania Dutchman,* beginning in 1957, and later for the *Pennsylvania Folklife* magazine. His photo essays on the Amish appeared regularly until 1961.[19]

Then from 1961-1965 Tortora also worked to supply professional photography for the Pennsylvania Folklife Society's public events, documenting significant activities and personalities at the Folk Festival and the Harvest Frolic. His work was showcased in the summer Special Festival Issues of *Pennsylvania Folklife,* and his color photos were also central to the Festival's publicity campaigns and annual promotional brochures. The Society supplied Tortora's photography with their press releases to local and national media outlets, and this is how images of Milton Hill found their way into some national newspapers like the *New York Times* on Sunday, June 17, 1962. The article featured the classic image of Milton Hill in his studio, and it is likely that this photograph was taken at the same time as a number of other widely-circulated images of Milton at work

1966 Kutztown Folk Festival promotional brochure advertising the 17th annual event and featuring Penny Wood of Ocean Grove, New Jersey gazing at the work of Milton J. Hill in a photograph by Vincent R. Tortora of Manheim, Lancaster County. Images of Milton's work would continue to play a central role in the Festival's advertising even up to the 1990s, long after he retired from the festival in 1968. *Kutztown Folk Festival Archive, Pennsylvania German Cultural Heritage Center, Kutztown University.*

which appeared in local publications such as the *Berks Historical Review,* the Allentown *Morning Call*, and the *Reading Eagle* newspaper.

Sometime in 1963 Tortora produced a series of staged publicity photos of Milton Hill and Penny Wood, a student at Kutztown State College and Festival volunteer from Ocean Grove, New Jersey, who posed with Milton's barn star in a patterned "prairie"-style dress and sunbonnet, which had become standard garb in Festival's second decade of operation. Against a colorful backdrop of Milton's stars leaning against a snowfence at the perimeter of the Festival parking lot, the two are seated on wooden chairs and appear to be discussing the artwork, while Milton pretends to paint with an oversized dry brush. In another shot in the same series, the volunteer in the sunbonnet examines one of Milton's colorful stars. Images from this photo shoot appeared on the cover of the advance brochure advertising the 17th annual Festival in 1966, as well as a series of postcards, and a full-page image in the Kutztown Borough's *Sesqui-Centennial Commemorative Book* published in 1965.[21]

Despite the staged nature of these photographs, Tortora's series of Milton Hill captures rare details of the artist in his final years at the Festival. The diversity of geometric forms and colors displayed in his work by this point in his career is unparalleled. The unique character and magnanimity of the artist comes through in his focus and poise, and the formality of his distinctive work attire. These views of Milton capture the colorful spirit of his final years at the festival before his retirement from public events in 1968.

A staged vignette of Milton J. Hill painting at the Kutztown Folk Festival in 1963, while festival volunteer and Kutztown State College student Penny Wood of Ocean Grove, New Jersey watches the process, taken by Festival photographer Vincent R. Tortora of Manheim. *Courtesy of the Kutztown Sesqui-Centennial Publication Committee & The Kutztown Area Historical Society.*

Milton J. and Gertrude D. (Strausser) Hill celebrated their 55th Anniversary on November 6, 1965 at the Abraham Lincoln Hotel's Lounge with a party thrown by their four living children Jacob W. Hill, Milton D. Hill, Ellen E. (Hill) Heffner, and Esther L. (Hill) Derr, and their spouses (their eldest son, John L. was already deceased), along with 13 grandchildren, eight great grandchildren, and dozens of family and friends were in attendance. *Courtesy of Lee S. Heffner & Family.*

CHAPTER VI

An Artist's Epilogue

In the years following his retirement from the Kutztown Folk Festival at the age of 81, Milton continued to paint from his studio in the henhouse on the Hill farm, but stayed out of the public spotlight. Customers continued to visit his studio to purchase his work and hunt for antiques, while he would alternate between painting and resting on the old rocking chair by his ornate cast iron stove. He got many questions about his flashy 1866 "Magnet Egg" stove produced by Orr, Painter & Co. of Reading, but he refused to sell it, asking rhetorically, "what would I use to heat my studio?"[1] Eventually, due to a number of health-related factors, Milton began to slow considerably in the creation of his original artwork. When visitors arrived at the farm to admire his work, he was just as likely to be napping on the couch as out in his studio, and Gertrude would assist customers if Milton was unavailable.

His youngest daughter Esther (Hill) Derr, who lived across the street from the farm with her husband Harold, and two daughters, Dorian and Lisa, had been helping her father with his painting even during his final years of the festival.[2] As Milton's health had begun to decline, Esther took on a greater role, painting the stars that her father carefully laid-out with his compass and scribe. Esther is the unsung artist behind a number of Milton's final pieces, some of which stayed close within the family. Her technical skill as a painter was indistinguishable from her father's, and although she took great joy in helping Milton, she never personally pursued the art any further when Milton finally gave up painting sometime around the year 1970.

That same year, on October 12, Milton and Gertrude deeded the farm and all of its acreage to their son Jacob W. Hill, with the arrangement that they would be allowed to remain on the farm as long as they were able.[3]

Just less than a month later on November 6, Milton and Gertrude celebrated their 60th wedding anniversary, and a party was held at the home of Esther and Harold Derr, with 75 people in attendance, including Milton and Gertrude's thirteen grandchildren and sixteen great-grandchildren. The couple had celebrated their previous milestone of 55 years with great fanfare at the Abraham

A complicated star, layout by Milton J. Hill, and painted by his youngest daughter Esther L. (Hill) Derr. Esther assisted her father with *Courtesy of Dorian (Derr) Fetherolf & Family.*

As the ever supportive and loving wife, Gertrude, along with her youngest daughter Esther, cared for Milton in his final years, as his mobility decreased and he spent a significant amount of his time resting. On a cold Sunday afternoon, the day after New Year's day 1972, Gertrude prepared Milton his favorite lunch, a Lebanon bologna and cheese sandwich, and took it upstairs to where Milton was resting.[5] A short time later, she found that Milton had peacefully passed away, in the same upstairs bedroom on the west side of the house where he had been born 84 years, 9 months, and 9 days ago.

It was bitter cold on Thursday, January 6, when 177 friends, family, and neighbors gathered to celebrate the life of Milton Hill at Zion's United Church of Christ in Windsor Castle. Arrangements were made by Burkey and Spacht Funeral Home in Hamburg, and two ministers representing both of the family's denominational affiliations officiated, with Rev. Dr. Herbert B. Zechman from the U. C. C. and Rev. Thomas J. Keener from the Lutheran congregation.[5] The readings for the service were from Psalm 23, and the Gospel of John, chapter 14: "Let not your heart be troubled: ye believe in God, believe also in me. In my Father's house are many mansions: if it were not so, I would have told you. I go to prepare a place for you..." The congregation joined together in singing the hymn "God Be With You Till We Meet Again."

Top: Milton J. and Gertrude D. (Strausser) Hill on their 60th wedding anniversary party at the home of Harold J. and Esther (Hill) Derr. *Courtesy of Lee S. Heffner & Family.*
Bottom: Gertrude and Milton Hill, with Gertrude's sister Sallie (Strausser) Hoffa, in front of the bake oven on the Hill Farm, ca.1970. *Courtesy of Lee S. Heffner & Family.*

Lincoln Hotel's formal English Lounge on North 5th Street, Reading.[4]

Milton and Gertrude continued to live on the farm, with the dairy operation still under Gertrude's management, and with much assistance from Esther and Harold Derr who lived just across the street, as well as the whole extended family.

There was snow on the ground as the casket was placed by the graveside by pall bearers William T. Hill, Robert M. Hill, Lee S. Heffner, Daniel T. Hill, Milton's grandsons, and the husbands of granddaughters, Phares W. Fry and Allen J. Billig.[6] As was customary, those gathered closed the service with a parting hymn by the graveside "Asleep in

Jesus." Milton was laid to rest in the old Union Cemetery along side his father and mother, and great-grandparents, and among four generations of the Hill family.

The years that followed were difficult for Gertrude, as she continued to live alone on the farm and operate the dairy until 1977. Gertrude was not only the proprietor of the farm at this time, but she also served as the primary milker until 1975, a task which she continued to do by hand. Even at the age of 80, friends and relatives continued to remark that she could milk faster by hand than anyone they knew. As the farm operation was much too big to handle entirely on her own, she continued to receive additional help from family and neighbors, and employed Chester Mull as the farmhand, who lived at the neighboring farm of Ernest and Dorothy (Mull) Lukens, his uncle and aunt. Chester became the Hill Farm's primary milker after 1975, and helped on the farm through its final years under Gertrude's management.[7]

As the years continued to roll by, Gertrude required more consistent care and assistance in daily life. Initially during this transition, she spent her days on the farm, but her evenings and night in the home of her son-in-law and daughter, Harold and Esther Derr, who lived just across the road. Eventually, however, she had to make the difficult decision to leave the farm altogether. The farm had been her home, a property she shaped and cared for since marrying Milton in 1910.

Gertrude cried when she had to sell her cows in 1977, knowing that she had to move from the farm permanently and could no longer care for them.[8] She had managed this herd of cows for 65 years, in everything from milking to breeding, delivering to weaning, over many generations. These cows were members of the family, sustaining the farm as a viable business, nourishing many generations of the Hill family, and even supporting the artistry of Milton Hill.

Gertrude passed away on Thursday, October 19, 1978, around 10 o'clock in the morning surrounded by members of her family, including her two daughters Esther and Ellen, as well as her daughter-in-law Agnes. 205 people from the *Freindschaft* gathered for the viewing on the evening of Sunday, October 22, and for the funeral service the following afternoon at Zion United Church of Christ, with Rev. Peter S. Shults and Rev. Lynn L. Langkamer officiating.[9] Gertrude was laid to rest next to her husband Milton Hill in Zion Union cemetery.

Today, the farm, still in the hands of the Hill family, lies quiet. Milton's and his son John's stars no longer shine forth from the barn, but lie dormant under coats of white paint, with only the barest of visual impressions in just the right angle of sunlight.

Nevertheless, nearly five decades after Milton's passing from this world, his art continues to live on. Barns graced by his brush are still visible in Perry and Windsor Townships, and throughout the region, where his work continues to inspire new generations of artists to carry on the tradition. Not only have Milton's stars been repainted time and time again, but his work has provided the impetus for others to follow in his footsteps and improvise—a process that brings vibrant patterns of seemingly infinite varieties to life with each new generation.

Above: A Milton Hill star, scribed by Milton and painted by his daughter Esther L. (Hill) Derr sometime around 1970. *Courtesy of Dorian (Derr) Fetherolf & Family.*

A well-maintained barn originally painted by Milton J. Hill, and repainted sometime in the last 20 years. The barn is owned by descendants of Milton Hill, and is located outside of Virginville, Berks County. *Photographic Survey of Decorated Barns, Patrick J. Donmoyer 2007-2020.*

CHAPTER VII

An Open-Air Gallery

Historic & Contemporary Barns Painted by Milton J. Hill

Perhaps the greatest testament to the impact of Milton Hill's artistry on the region's culture is the persistent presence of his work in the local landscape. Especially in Northern Berks County, historic barns still bear the evidence of his personal interactions with scribe and brushwork. Although many of these have long ago been repainted by farm owners and artists, his work persists as part of a continually maintained living tradition.

Some of Milton's earliest works are no longer visible in the landscape and only remain recorded in period photographs ranging from the early to the middle of the twentieth century. Photographers like Wallace A. Dietrich (1853-1909) of Kutztown took a series of at least two photographs of the artist Milton Hill at work, although many more may also exist.

In the 1930s and 40s, William E. Ferrell (1870-1949), founder and president of the Easton Car and Construction Company, turned to documenting hundreds of decorated barns in his late career, especially in the Lehigh Valley. Ferrell also ventured into northern Berks, where he documented several barns painted by Milton Hill.

Ferrell's photography inspired additional work by architect Charles H. Dornbusch, who received a Langley Fellowship in 1941 from the American Institute of Architects to document and study Pennsylvania Barns. Many of his photographic negatives were donated to the Historic American Buildings Survey at the Library of Congress, and some of these include barns by Milton Hill.[1] Along with fellow architect John K. Heyl (1906-2011) Dornbusch co-authored a study entitled *Pennsylvania German Barns*, which was published in 1958 by the Pennsylvania German Folklore Society.

Still other avid photographers of decorated barns from the mid-twentieth century include the Allentown school teacher Guy F. Reinert (1892-1962), and Henry K. Deischer (1867-1951), a senior associate at the State Museum. Their mid-twentieth century views of Berks and Lehigh

Above: A star inspired by Milton Hill's earliest childhood watercolor paintings ca. 1899, and reproduced on the Kistler-Snyder Barn near Lenhartsville, Berks County by Eric Claypoole, Joanna Blessing, and Patrick Donmoyer in 2014. *Survey of Decorated Barns, Patrick J. Donmoyer 2007-2020.*

County decorated barns were published extensively as part of the Kutztown Folk Festival's 1950s programs, along with essays by Dr. Alfred L. Shoemaker, including some by Milton Hill in the vicinity of Virginville.[2]

These early photographs are highly significant in capturing rare views of the regional landscape, yet they are second only to the barns themselves, which combine agricultural function and cultural expression in one monumental form. These historic barns persist long after the original builders, farmers and decorators are only a memory, enticing new generations of barn star painters to take up the brush, ascend the ladder, and revitalize the landscape once more.

The following pages feature a series of open-air galleries of regional barns painted by Milton Hill or influenced by him that were depicted in historic and contemporary views. Many of these historic barns bear witness to the work of many artists throughout the decades, and demonstrate the collaborative spirit embodied by the painting crews of the past and present. Farm owners, artists, commercial painters, and barn owners have all played an important role in decorating these barns, and rarely is anything done "solo." Likewise, many artists did not sign their work, and relied instead upon the visual recognition of their signature styles and patterns.

No one more epitomizes this approach than Milton Hill. Nevertheless, a number of painters who followed in his footsteps produced work that is so similar in form, that today there can be some confusion about whether a barn star is truly the original work of the master himself, one of his helpers, or just another artist inspired by Milton Hill.

Milton's eldest son John L. Hill (1911-1963), is one of the most notable painters who worked in the style of his father. John was best known for his murals of farm scenes and livestock, but he also painted stars in the years between the time when his father was no longer climbing ladders and the time of his accidental death in the summer of 1963.

Another barn painter who worked with Milton Hill was Harry L. Adam (1915-2005) of Edenburg, who began painting as an apprentice in 1936, and later ran a prolific painting crew of his own that decorated many local barns throughout Northern Berks.

Harry Adam's signature star designs were very similar to Milton Hill's work, and are only distinguishable by their simplified border, formed by a series of arcs overlapping by half, rather than by the one-fourth ratio that Milton used in his signature pattern. Thus Harry's borders were intricate but narrower than Milton's. These subtleties were a both a nod to Milton's work, as well as a way for Harry Adam to set his work apart. The difference in style is also emblematic of the way the artistic tradition lends itself to both

An original Milton Hill Star on a straw shed located near Onyx Cave, repainted by Johnny P. Claypoole of Lenhartsville in 1995. This was the last barn star painted by Johnny Claypoole before passing the torch to his son Eric Claypoole. *Survey of Decorated Barns, Patrick J. Donmoyer 2007-2020.*

Contemporary and historic farmscape views of Del-Jame farms, owned by James H. and Delores Adam, near Virginville, featuring stars by Milton J. Hill on the shed, and livestock murals on the barn and shed by John L. Hill. The 8-pointed stars on the barn were likely added by Harry L. Adam of Edenburg, who repainted the Milton Hill Stars sometime in the mid-1960s.

Above: Photo by Dave Fooks for the Kutztown Folk Festival and the Hex Tour Association.

Below: Photo by William E. Ferrell of Easton, ca. 1940. Note the absence of the 8-pointed stars on the barn. *Pennsylvania German Cultural Heritage Center, Kutztown University.*

repetition and innovation with each new generation.³

Harry Adam was also a tax collector for Windsor Township for 24 years between 1946-1970, as well as a dealer in furs and hides, and in 1953, Adam opened a paint store.⁴ His store stocked all of the paints, oils, and pigments needed by artists such as the barn star painter Johnny P. Claypoole (1921-2004) of Lenhartsville. Claypoole began his career as the apprentice of commercial hex sign artist Johnny Ott (1890-1964), proprietor of the Lenhartsville Hotel. Although Ott never painted on any barns, and only produced what he called "hex signs" on commercial signboard, Claypoole went on to paint dozens of barns in the area, applying the technical painting skills that he learned to the historic surfaces of the barn. Claypoole repainted many stars including ones by Milton Hill. Johnny Claypoole had mostly painted barns in Northern Berks, below the Blue Mountain, but he also reached beyond into other parts of Southeastern Pennsylvania. region.⁵ His work was also later commissioned for installations at the Smithsonian Institution in 1969, the British Embassy, and the Philadelphia Zoo, and featured in widespread publications such as the National Geographic and the *New York Times*.

The very last job that Johnny Claypoole had painted directly on a barn was in 1995, when he repainted a star on a straw shed original by Milton Hill on a barn near Onyx Cave, Perry Township, while his son Eric A. Claypoole (b. 1960) completed the stars on the upper gable and forebay of the barn. Eric had been helping his father paint barns since 1972, the very same year that Milton Hill passed away. Since that time, the painting of barns has become a passion and vocation for Eric, who has followed in his father's footsteps in both painting barns and painting modern hex signs in the style of Johnny Ott and Johnny Claypoole on commercial signboard.

At the time of the release of this publication, Eric has been painting barns for nearly 50 years, with the greatest number of barns having been painted in the last 25 years. It is unknown how many barns Eric has painted over the last half-century, but the known number currently exceeds 80, and it is expected that he will complete over 100 barns in his lifetime—a truly monumental achievement exceeding all other known barn star painters. Eric has repainted numerous original Hill Stars, and has created new designs inspired by Milton Hill visible today on dozens of additional barns in Northern Berks and throughout the region.

Along with the efforts of other individual farmers, painters, and homeowners, we can see that Milton Hill's creative influence as a painter has not diminished since his passing, but interest in his work has continued to grow and shape the Pennsylvania Dutch landscape and folk culture.

An original Milton Hill Star on the barn at the Sunday Farm near Virginville, repainted by Johnny Claypoole sometime in the 1980s, ca. 2008. The barn was later repainted again by Eric Claypoole in 2011. *Survey of Decorated Barns, Patrick J. Donmoyer 2007-2020.*

Two views of a historic barn in Maiden Creek Township, bearing Milton Hill Stars, present location unknown.
Above: Photo by Charles H. Dornbusch, ca. 1940. Historic American Buildings Survey, Library of Congress.

Below: Photo by William E. Ferrell, ca. 1940. *Pennsylvania German Cultural Heritage Center, Kutztown University.*

Above: A 1940s farmscape view at the site of one of the present-day Schock Farms in Tilden Township, photograph by William E. Ferrell. *Pennsylvania German Cultural Heritage Center, Kutztown University.*

Below: A present-day view of the Schock Barn's original Milton Hill Stars, repainted by Eric Claypoole of Lenhartsville, and his nephew Billy Reidel in 2008. *Survey of Decorated Barns, Patrick J. Donmoyer 2007-2020.*

Top: A series of four Milton Hill stars on the Schock Barn in Tilden Township, showing an alternating sequence of yellow and black for each star across the length the barn, creating a subtle variation. Decorative cutout wooden lattice work around the windows gives the barn a distinctive Western Berks County appearance.

Middle: Details of the stars in the process of being repainted by Eric Claypoole and his nephew Billy Reidel in 2008.

Bottom: A classic Milton Hill Star in Tilden Township, captured in the process of being repainted by artist Eric Claypoole in 2008.

Survey of Decorated Barns, Patrick J. Donmoyer 2007-2020.

Top & Middle: Views of a barn painted by Milton Hill, location unknown, ca. 1940. Photograph taken by William E. Ferrell of Easton. *Pennsylvania German Cultural Heritage Center, Kutztown University.*

Bottom: Photograph of a barn painted by Milton J. Hill, located near Shartlesville, Berks County, taken by Henry K. Deisher, Kutztown Folk Festival Program, 1950.

Top: Leiby-Maleski Barn, Windsor Township, Berks County, featuring repainted Milton Hill stars, with detailed view (middle-left) of the stars geometry. *Survey of Decorated Barns, Patrick J. Donmoyer 2007-2020.*

Bottom: Two Milton Hill stars from a barn near Onyx Cave, Perry Township, Berks County, with a closeup (middle-right) of an unusual Hill Star, featuring a lobed 8-petalled blossom in the very center, and an unusual border, possibly repainted. *Survey of Decorated Barns, Patrick J. Donmoyer 2007-2020.*

Above: The decorated barn at the Sunday Farm near Virginville, Berks County. The barn was built by slate-quarry owner and stone carver Jacob Leiby (1798-1884), and was originally decorated by Milton Hill sometime in the early 20th century. The stars were repainted by Johnny Claypoole in the 1980s, and recently repainted by Eric Claypoole of Lenhartsville in 2011. *Survey of Decorated Barns, Patrick J. Donmoyer 2007-2020.*

Opposite: Details of the repainting process of the Milton Hill Stars by Eric Claypoole at the Sunday Farm in 2011. *Survey of Decorated Barns, Patrick J. Donmoyer 2007-2020.*

Left: A view of the old weathered "ghost" of one of Milton Hill's stars at the Sunday Farm, which was given three coats of paint prior to being restored by Eric Claypoole in 2011. The solid coat of while allows the differential solar weathering to be clearly visible in certain lighting. One can see the complete geometry of Milton Hill's star layout, including the intricate layering of the star burst, and the border of interlaced arcs. The ghost was used as a template to repaint the star following Milton Hill's original design. These stars on the Sunday barn are 7 feet in diameter, and the central star is more intricate than the outer two on either side. This is a common arrangement for Milton Hill, who often reserved the central star on the barn for his signature striped border. *Survey of Decorated Barns, Patrick J. Donmoyer 2007-2020.*

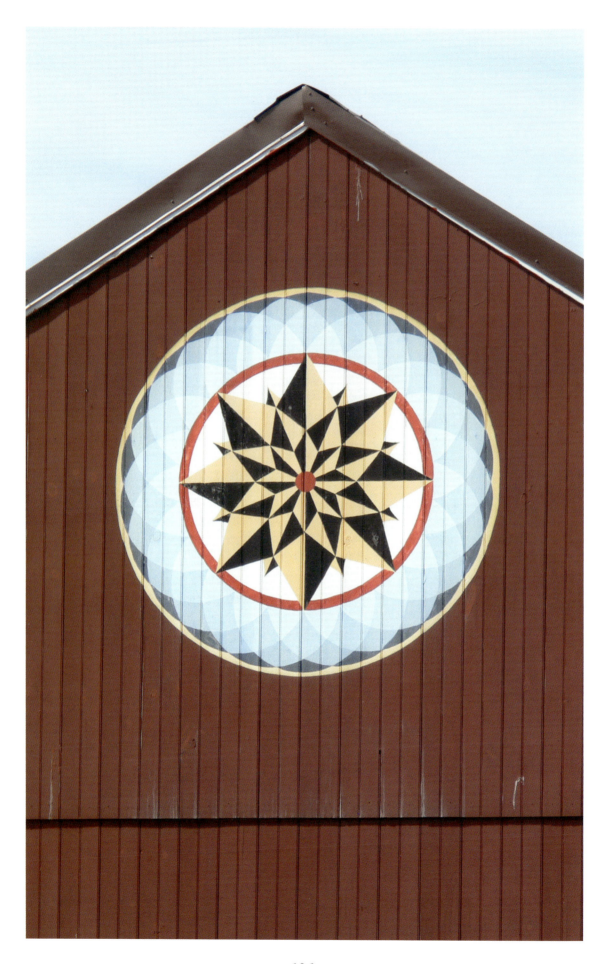

 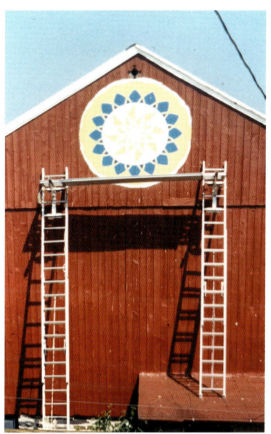

Above: Two views of the step by step repainting of the barn in the late 1980s by sign painter, artist, and musician Jack Murray of Landis Store. *Courtesy of Jack Murray.*

Below: A late 1990s view of the completed Milton Hill Star repainted by Jack Murray located just outside of Virginville. *Courtesy of David Fooks, Hex Tour Association & Kutztown Folk Festival.*

Opposite: A recent repainting of the Milton Hill Star by Eric Claypoole of Lenhartsville and Andrew Shirk of Hamburg after the siding was replaced in 2018. *Survey of Decorated Barns, Patrick J. Donmoyer 2007-2020.*

Above: A classic Milton Hill Star on the upper gable end of a barn in Ruscombmanor Township, Berks County, which shows signs of having been repainted perhaps by Harry Adam of Edenburg. Other stars on the forebay and bank doors of the barn show the narrow border characteristic of the work of Harry Adam, suggesting that he may have added to the decorative scheme of the barn at the time he repainted the Milton Hill Star on the upper gable.

Below: A Hill Star variation with a border in the style of Harry Adam, with only two layers of border scallops, and a simplified inner border.

Survey of Decorated Barns, Patrick J. Donmoyer 2007-2020.

Above: A Tilden Township barn originally painted by Milton J. Hill, and repainted in 2013 by Eric Claypoole of Lenhartsville and Patrick J. Donmoyer. This particular star pattern is one of Milton Hill's early variations, featuring the classic eight-pointed star burst, but lacking his signature interlaced border. Variations like this appear on several barns throughout the region.

Middle: A progression of repainting in several stages, showing each color layer of the design. The ghost of the original design is visible, showing that at least one star on the barn had additional points, but the designs were standardized when they were repainted.

Bottom: Eric Claypoole looks out over the barnyard while completing the red scallops along the interior border. Two five-foot stars on the upper gable end of the barn are visible from US Route 78 between Hamburg and Shartlesville, Berks County.

Survey of Decorated Barns, Patrick J. Donmoyer 2007-2020.

Above: A barn in Hereford Township, Berks County, likely painted by Harry L. Adam (1915-2005) of Edenburg in his signature style, inspired by the work of Milton J. Hill. Adam's stars feature similar elements to the Hill Star, but differ in terms of the starburst layouts, central pinwheels, and simplified borders. Harry Adam was one of many painters who worked with Milton Hill on his painting crew, and served as an apprentice in 1936. *Survey of Decorated Barns, Patrick J. Donmoyer 2007-2020.*

Left: One of Harry Adam's last stars painted on commercial signboard, on a barn in Greenwich Township, Berks County. Below: A comparison of two Harry Adam stars, including one from Greenwich Township (left) and from Hereford Township (right). *Survey of Decorated Barns, Patrick J. Donmoyer 2007-2020.*

Above: An LP of Pennsylvania Dutch songs and folklore by Phares H. Hertzog (1868-1935), featuring the Friendly Acres barn owned and painted by Melvin S. Lonergan (1928-2010) of Tilden Township, Berks County. Melvin ran a septic company, and had been an apprentice painter under Milton J. Hill. *Arcadia Inc. 1973.*

Below: The stars, visible along Route 61, were repainted in 2010 by Eric Claypoole of Lenhartsville. *Survey of Decorated Barns, Patrick J. Donmoyer 2007-2020.*

Top: The 1819 Kistler-Snyder Barn, is located in Greenwich Township, just north of Lenhartsville. The stars were repainted in the fall of 2014 by Eric Claypoole, with help from two friends. The barn stars were based on Milton J. Hill's earliest stars, which he painted ca. 1899 when still in the one-room schoolhouse at Virginville.

Above: The barn also features one of the earliest barn star date boards in the whole region from 1819, and was repainted by Eric Claypoole in 2004.

Left: Eric Claypoole finishes one of the barn stars.

Opposite, top: The barn painting in process, with ladders set up for the painters, and the barnyard wall still under construction.

Opposite, bottom (clockwise from the top left): A completed star; Eric Claypoole applies touch-up; Patrick J. Donmoyer paints the first color layer on one star; Joanna Blessing completes a coat of yellow.

Survey of Decorated Barns, Patrick J. Donmoyer 2007-2020.

Milton Hill Stars produced by Johnny Claypoole (1921-2004) of Lenhartsville, Berks County. Although Johnny was primarily a painter on commercial signboard, he also painted a number of significant barns in the region, and some were inspired by the work of barn star artist Milton J. Hill, and are still visible in the local landscape.

Top (Left): A stylized interpretation of the Hill Star, featuring a simplified border, by Johnny Claypoole, located on the upper gable of a barn in Earl Township, Berks County; (Right) Detail of a weathered door painted by Johnny Claypoole, located on a drive-through corncrib in District Township, Berks County.

Bottom: A pair of Milton Hill Stars by Johnny Claypoole, painted on a barn in Lower Macungie, Lehigh County.

Survey of Decorated Barns, Patrick J. Donmoyer 2007-2020.

Above: A Milton Hill Star by Johnny Claypoole, created to fit a circular recess formerly occupied by a large date board on an early nineteenth century barn in the Oley Valley. The star was later repainted by Eric Claypoole.

Below: Another view of the same barn, being embellished with four Milton Hill Stars by Eric Claypoole in 2013. *Survey of Decorated Barns, Patrick J. Donmoyer 2007-2020.*

Above: A modern Hill Star in progress on a barn in Greenwich Township. *Courtesy of Eric Claypoole.*

Middle: A view of the finished star (right) and its companion, also based on a star pattern historically used by Milton Hill. *Survey of Decorated Barns, Patrick J. Donmoyer 2007-2020.*

Bottom (Left): A star inspired by Milton Hill, painted by Eric Claypoole on the wagon shed at the Ontelaunee Hotel in Virginville; (Right): A Milton Hill Star by Eric Claypoole on the farm in Windsor Township formerly belonging to Oscar Adam, who painted with Milton Hill in the first decades of the twentieth century. *Survey of Decorated Barns, Patrick J. Donmoyer 2007-2020.*

A Richmond Township barn, painted by Eric Claypoole in 2001 with two central patterns inspired by Milton J. Hill. This barn was the first to be painted through grant funding supported by the collaborative efforts between the Hex Tour Association, the Kutztown Folk Festival, and the Pennsylvania German Cultural Heritage Center at Kutztown University. *Survey of Decorated Barns, Patrick J. Donmoyer 2007-2020.*

Above: A Richmond Township Barn originally decorated by Milton Hill in the 1950s, but later modernized with the addition of metal siding. Four Milton Hill Stars on sign board were painted by Eric Claypoole in 2010.

Below: A postcard of the Richmond Township barn featured above, showing the original stars by Milton J. Hill. *Pennsylvania German Cultural Heritage Center, Kutztown University.*

Left: A remnant of an original Milton Hill Star enclosed within a strawshed addition put on the barn sometime around 1920. The barn star was painted around, covering Milton Hill's classic border. Located in Greenwich Township, Berks County. *Survey of Decorated Barns, Patrick J. Donmoyer 2007-2020.*

Right: An original Milton Hill disk, located on a barn in Perry Township, Berks County. The design is a seven-pointed star, which is nearly identical to the original seven-pointed stars presumably painted by Milton's father John M. Hill, visible only as ghosts today on the barn at the Hill Farm. Historic views of these stars are included on page 25 of this book. *Survey of Decorated Barns, Patrick J. Donmoyer 2007-2020.*

Above: A star inspired by Milton J. Hill, painted by Patrick J. Donmoyer in 2014 on a the historic barn of Larry and Linda Glass outside of Douglassville, Berks County. *Survey of Decorated Barns, Patrick J. Donmoyer 2007-2020.*

CHAPTER VIII

Inspired Artistry

A Gallery of Contemporary Art in the Spirit of Milton J. Hill

Above: A Milton Hill Star painted on weathered barn siding by folk artist and hex sign painter Ivan E. Hoyt in May of 2019, on display at the Kutztown Folk Festival. *Courtesy of Ivan E. Hoyt & Family.*

Opposite: A "Ghost Project" by Eric Claypoole, featuring a Milton Hill Star painted on rough bare wood, and allowed to weather in open air for several years. Without a background coat, the star weathers rapidly, and all exposed wood begins to recede in just a few years due to the action of the sun and the stripping of the wood fiber by insects such as wasps for paper nests. The painted areas are protected from the solar rays, producing a profound differential relief over time. *Courtesy of Eric Claypoole.*

Above: Seven hand-painted variations of the Milton Hill Star by Andrew D. Shirk of Hamburg, 2018-2020, and one house blessing with a Milton Hill border. *Courtesy of Andrew Shirk.*

Above: A wide variety of stars inspired by Milton Hill, painted by Eric Claypoole of Lenhartsville, including (top right) a shot overlooking the hills

Above Left: An elaborate Hill Star pattern on a barn in Rockland Township, Berks County, composed in an unusual format, consisting of painted wooden cutouts arranged in layers. Artist unknown. *Survey of Decorated Barns, Patrick J. Donmoyer 2007-2020.*

Above Right: A Hill Star painted by Douglas E. Rontz (1957-2016) of Jim Thorpe, Pennsylvania, as a commission for Milton Hill's granddaughter, Dorian (Derr) Fetherolf, containing the adapted inscription in Pennsylvania Dutch: "You are my pretty little girl." *Courtesy of Dorian (Derr) Fetherolf & Family.*

Below: Two multi-layered starbursts inspired by the work of Milton J. Hill, painted by former Berks County resident Tim Herring of Virginia, 2020. *Courtesy of Tim Herring.*

Left: Ivan E. Hoyt's signature tree of life design with two pairs of distelfinks, surrounded by an intricate geometric border inspired by the classic borders used by Milton J. Hill. *Courtesy of Ivan E. Hoyt & Family, 2020.*

Right: A contemporary interpretation of a Milton Hill starburst pattern, incorporating a bold color scheme of red, black and goldenrod yellow, and a distinctive scalloped border articulated with five-pointed stars. *Courtesy of Ivan E. Hoyt & Family, 2016.*

Above: Two examples of star variations inspired by Milton Hill, painted by Patrick J. Donmoyer in 2009 and 2020, featuring a unique condensed adaptation of the Hill border

Beginning in 2009, the Pennsylvania State Grange initiated a statewide Heritage Quilt Trail, which encouraged all local Granges to develop quilt squares reflecting their regional community identities. These painted squares are displayed on the exteriors of Grange Halls throughout the Commonwealth, including the Virginville Community Grange #1832, which featured designs honoring the Virginville artist Milton J. Hill. All Grange quilt squares were required to use straight-lines only, and the Milton Hill Star was adapted accordingly by Eric Claypoole of Lenhartsville. *Survey of Decorated Barns, Patrick J. Donmoyer 2007-2020.*

Dietrich's Meats and Country Store in Krumsville, Berks County features a Milton Hill Star as their company logo, and the design appears on all of their products and advertising. Started in 1957, the company is known today for their emphasis on regional Pennsylvania Dutch traditional foodways, specializing not only in culturally significant meat products, but a wide variety of other quality foods. The company's proprietor is Verna (Leiby) Dietrich, who grew up on the farm established by her ancestor Jacob Leiby of Virginville, as well as another neighboring Leiby Farm which spans Windsor and Perry Townships. Both farms feature barn stars originally painted by Milton J. Hill sometime in the 1940s.

Courtesy of Dietrich's Meats and Country Store

The historic Dreibelbis Station Bridge, spanning the Maiden Creek and Windsor and Greenwich townships, is one of five historic covered bridges in Berks County, and one of the longest single-span covered bridges in the United States. For at least a half-century the bridge has featured a barn star above each entry, and the earliest of these were painted in the 1960s by Johnny Ott. Johnny Claypoole replaced Ott's stars sometime in the 1970s, and a second time in 1997. Eric Claypoole painted new stars to replace his father's for the bridge in 2020, and these featured Milton Hill Stars in honor of the artist's influence in the region. As a subtle nod to Milton Hill's style, Eric even swirled the central circle of the star by hand, just as Milton Hill had done on all of his signs produced on commercial signboard in the 1950s and 60s. After a more than one year restoration project supported by a grant from the Nation Historic Covered Bridge Preservation Program, the bridge reopened to traffic on August 21, 2020. *Survey of Decorated Barns, Patrick J. Donmoyer 2007-2020.*

Above: Annual demonstrations at the Kutztown Folk Festival by the Pennsylvania German Cultural Heritage Center include live collaborative painting sessions in order to produce four barn star panels included in the Festival Quilt Auction. The painting team from 2019 included (clockwise from top left) Andrew D. Shirk, Sarah E. Edris, Eric A. Claypoole, and Patrick J. Donmoyer. Opposite: Milton Hill-inspired stars painted at the Kutztown Folk Festival Barn Star Demonstrations. 2016-2019.

Photos by Naomi E. Pauley, Pennsylvania German Cultural Heritage Center, Kutztown University

Top: A Milton Hill Star created for display at the 2018 Kutztown Folk Festival by Patrick J. Donmoyer and Sarah E. Edris of the Pennsylvania German Cultural Heritage Center, Kutztown University, 2018.

Bottom: Two star patterns recreated from historic photographs of Milton Hill's work by Sarah E. Edris (right) and Sarah E. Edris and Katherine M. Wash (left) of the Pennsylvania German Cultural Heritage Center, Kutztown University in 2018.

Above: Three historic Milton Hill designs painted by Sarah E. Edris of Mohrsville, at the Pennsylvania German Cultural Heritage Center, Kutztown University for display at the Kutztown Folk Festival as part of a retrospective exhibition in 2018.

Milton J. Hill hanging a barn star disk, likely a staged photograph at the Hill Barn by Vincent R. Tortora. *Courtesy of Lee S. Heffner & Family.*

ENDNOTES

CHAPTER I

1. For more on the origins of the Hill Family of Heuchelheim, see Burgert, Annette Kunselman. 2000. *Palatine Origins of Some Pennsylvania Pioneers.* Myerstown, PA: AKB Publications, 158.

2. Strassburger, Ralph Beaver & John William Hinke. 1992. *Pennsylvania German Pioneers.* Camden, ME: Picton Press, Vol I: xviii.

3. Annette Burgert addresses the family's records in Heuchelheim (1709-1719), as well as the same family's appearance in American records in Pennsylvania beginning in 1739), pp. 158-159. There are several conflicting theories about precisely when the Hill family arrived in Pennsylvania. Some have suggested that the lapse of family records in Heuchelheim following the birth of the son Johann Phillip Hill in 1719 suggests that the family left within a year or so of 1720. Others speculate that the Hill family left Heuchelheim and settled near Meisenheim, where a daughter was born August 30 1726 to a Jacob and Anna Elizabetha Hill, and baptized at the Meisenheim Lutheran Church September 4, 1726, by the name of Anna Maria. This is believed by some to be "Anna Maria Christina" who later married Johann Jacob Merkel (1729-1779) on December 18, 1750 at Moselem, Berks County. Furthermore a son Daniel was believed to have been born in Berks County in 1728, which suggests that the Hill Family arrived sometime between 1726 and 1728. Sources for this theory are generally lacking, aside from the mention of a Jacob and Anna Elizabetha in the Meisenheim Church records. Although there is no certainty that this is the same Hill family (there were many throughout the region), there remains much speculation on the subject on genealogical forums online. The current leading genealogist for the Hill family is Tim Conrad, of Ancest4.com, and we appreciate his discussion of the Hill family in preparation for this book.

4. Burgert 2000: 225-226.

5. Citation of Morton L. Montgomery in Meiser, George M. IX. 1998. *The Passing Scene XI.* Reading, PA: Reading Eagle Press.

6. Ibid.

7. Members of the Hill family moved to Western Pennsylvania, but earlier theories of the origins of the family are erroneous in: Beers, J. H. 1914. *Armstrong County, Pennsylvania: Her People, Past and Present*. Chicago: J. H. Beers & Co., 468-496.

8. Marriage record by Rev. John Casper Stoever on July 13, 1739, listed in *Early Lutheran Baptisms and Marriages in Southeastern Pennsylvania: The Records of John Casper Stoever from 1730-1779.* Baltimore: Genealogical Publishing Company, 1984, 57. For more information on the Lambsheim/Heuchelheim connection, see Burgert 158-159 & 225-226.

9. The original 1747 Hill land grant was photographed by members of the family, and the original is privately owned by a community member in the region. See also, Pennsylvania Historical & Museum Commission; Deed Book C-067: 468(1).

10. Pennsylvania Historical & Museum Commission; Records of the Office of the Comptroller General, RG-4; *Tax & Exoneration Lists, 1762-1794*; Microfilm Roll: 316.

11. The details of this division of the property from April 9, 1894 in Deed Book 0206: 0128, Berks County Recorder of Deeds.

12. This is the first-hand memory of Ellen Elizabeth (Hill) Heffner (1914-2004), recorded by her son Lee S. Heffner.

13. Trexler, Mark K. 1959. *The Lutheran Church in Berks County.* Kutztown, PA: Kutztown Publishing Company, 253.

14. Birth and baptismal certificate in the collection of the Pennsylvania German Cultural Heritage Center, Kutztown University.

15. The Pennsylvania Dutch language was so central to the home experience for the Hills, that in 1900 US Federal Census enumerator, Abraham F. Zuber, incorrectly listed both John M. Hill and Ellen E (Wanner) Hill, as being unable to speak English on the Twelfth Census of the United States.

16. One-room school house teacher at Virginville, Jeremiah P. Adam (1880-1966), known by Milton as "Jerry," was not much older than Milton himself. He is buried at the cemetery at Zion Reformed UCC Church, Perry Township. His role in encouraging Milton Hill is included in: DeChant, Alliene S. 1958. "Barn Sign Painter." *Historical Review of Berks County.* Spring XXIII(2): 54-55.

17. Zehner, Olive. 1953. "The Hills from Hamburg." *Pennsylvania Dutchman.* IV(11): 16, 13. Lancaster, PA: Pennsylvania Dutch Folklore Center, Franklin & Marshall College.

18. Milton J. Hill Ledger, Pennsylvania German Cultural Heritage Center, Kutztown University.

19. Letter in the personal collection of Lee S. Heffner, dated July 25, 1907, regarding U.S. Patent No. 857,879.

20. Kidd, H.S. 1923. *Lutherans in Berks County; Two Centuries of Continuous Organized Church Life 1723-1923.* Reading, PA: Reading Conference of the Evangelical Lutheran Ministerium of Pennsylvania, 417. Rev. Harry C. Kline's portrait is also included with a biographical sketch.

21. Gertrude's birth and baptismal certificate, penned on by G. A. J. Heimbach of Reading in Shoemakersville on June 11, 1895, spells her name as "Gerdie." Her confirmation certificate also includes her name as "Gertie," when she was confirmed at St. John's (Gernant's) Reformed Church in Ontelaunee on April 3, 1909.

ENDNOTES

CHAPTER II

1. The question of the chronological parameters have been hotly debated. For a history including examples from the eighteenth century through the present day, see Donmoyer, Patrick J. 2019. *Hex Signs: Sacred and Celestial Symbolism in Pennsylvania Dutch Barn Stars.* Kutztown: Pennsylvania German Cultural Heritage Center, Kutztown University. The dialog concerning the earliest stars was utterly changed in the early 2000s when early examples were discovered, and challenged the idea that barns were only painted after 1830. See Fooks, David. 2002. "In Search of America's Oldest Hex Signs," *Der Reggeboge.* 36(1):21–27; Fooks, David. 2003. "The History of Hex Signs." *The Pennsylvania German Review.* Fall 2003. Kutztown, PA: Pennsylvania German Cultural Heritage Center; compare with earlier studies, such as: Shoemaker, Alfred Lewis. 1953. Hex, No! Lancaster, PA: Pennsylvania Dutch Folklore Center, Franklin and Marshall College.

2. See Zehner 1953: 16, for an interview with Milton Hill, which includes a chronology of his life and work.

3. This was first told to me by Milton's youngest daughter, Esther (Hill) Derr in 2012. The only written source which appears to corroborate this idea is in a photo caption by Vincent Tortora, stating "Today, a few old-time "hex sign" painters still ply the trade which has frequently been in the same family for several generations. One of these is Milton Hill of Hamburg, PA., who represents the third generation." Tortora, Vincent R. 1966 & 1980. *Pennsylvania Dutch Hex Signs Illustrated in Natural Color: Their Origins, History, Usage, and Significance.* Manheim: Photo Arts Press.

4. Ibid. Zehner reports that the Samuel Hepner barn was the first barn to be painted with Milton Hill's signature stars. Zehner reports in 1953 that Milton began painting this design "over 40 years ago" and that Milton had been painting for over 50 years total. This suggests that his earliest work was located on Kohler Hill Road between Windsor Castle and Hamburg, the barn later burned and was modernized, leaving no trace of Milton's work.

5. Dr. Alfred Shoemaker documented dialect terms during field work in the late 1940s, and later published this research starting in 1950 in the Kutztown Folk Festival commemorative booklet. This classic essay was published under several editions and titles. See Shoemaker, Alfred L. 1953. *Hex, No!* Lancaster, PA: Pennsylvania Dutch Folklore Center, Franklin and Marshall College, and again in Shoemaker. 1955. *The Pennsylvania Barn.* Lancaster: Pennsylvania Dutch Folklore Center, Inc., Franklin and Marshall College.

6. See "Blumme & Schtanne: A Diversity of Forms" in Donmoyer, Patrick J. 2013. *Hex Signs: Myth and Meaning in Pennsylvania Dutch Barn Stars.* Kutztown, PA: Kutztown University of Pennsylvania; and Donmoyer 2017.

7. Yoder, Don & Thomas Graves. 2000. *Hex Signs: Pennsylvania Dutch Barn Symbols & Their Meaning.* 2nd Ed. Mechanicsburg, PA: Stackpole Books.

8. Nutting, Wallace. 1924. *Pennsylvania Beautiful.* Framingham, MA: Old America Company Publishers.

9. Ibid.

10. In the mid-twentieth century, scholars were divided into two camps, those who believed that the stars were strictly decorative, and those who believed that they were protective or symbolic, as explained in the "Scholars' War," Yoder & Graves 2000. A third, alternative perspective that the stars motifs are celestial representations is the primary theory undergirding views expressed in Donmoyer 2013 and Donmoyer 2019.

11. Donmoyer 2017 & 2013; Graves, Thomas E. 1984. *The Pennsylvania German Hex Sign: A Study in Folk Process.* University of Pennsylvania, dissertation.

12. Milton's hourly schedules and rotating crews of painters are documented in his ledger in the Milton Hill Collection at the Pennsylvania German Cultural Heritage Center, Kutztown University.

13. Zehner 1953: 16.

14. Milton J. Hill's ledger lists his purchased pigments used in the early twentieth century, and nineteenth-century barn painter Perry Ludwig's recipe is mentioned in Kauffman, Harry H. 1964. *Golden Stars on the Barn.* Privately published, no printing location.

15. Zehner 1953: 16.

16. Barr, Janet et al. 2007. *History of the Hamburg Area Volume II 1850-2000: 150 Years of Progress.* Kutztown, PA: Kutztown Publishing Co., 3.

17. Obituary for Wallace A. Dietrich. *The Morning Call.* Allentown. August 27, 1909.

18. Zehner 1953, 16.

19. This is likely George K. Hoch (1860-1948) of Richmond Township, Berks County, husband of Fannie S. (Hill) Hoch, buried at Zion Moselem Lutheran Church Cemetery, Berks County. PA Death Records, 1948.

20. Consumer Price Index Inflation Calculator, U.S. Department of Labor's Bureau of Labor Statistics.

21. Apparently some of these patterns were sold at the farm auction, following Gertrude's sale of the farm in 1972.

22. See: "The Ghost of a Star" in Donmoyer 2013.

23. This is explored in greater depth in Chapter IV: Magical Misconceptions.

ENDNOTES

CHAPTER III

1. This chapter on the life of Gertrude Hill is based upon a series of interviews with Lee S. Heffner 2009-2020, Esther (Hill) and Harold Derr in 2012 & 2019, and Dorian (Derr) Fetherolf in 2019 & 2020, and supplemented with additional sources.

2. *Pennsylvania Triennial Farm Census 1927*. PA State Archives, Pennsylvania Historical & Museum Commission.

3. A copy of the original land plat of the Hill Farm produced for Jacob Hill in 1870, based on the original 1739 grant, shows the property extending all the way to the Maiden Creek. A copy of this plat was maintained by Esther L. (Hill) and Harold J. Derr.

4. All of this is visible on an aerial photograph of the farm, taken in the mid-1950s, and explained by Lee S. Heffner in 2019-2020.

5. The outhouse is identical to other WPA outhouses documented in the region. These were part of widespread attempts to provide improved sanitation to agricultural communities following the Great Depression.

6. This word is a Pennsylvania Dutch diminutive form of the affectionate term for a cat "Puddy" also used in English.

7. A term common in Southeastern and Central Pennsylvania for any egg fried with a runny yolk, usually the equivalent of an over-easy egg.

8. Descriptions of Gertrude's garden were based on interviews with Lee S. Heffner and Dorian (Derr) Fetherolf in 2019.

CHAPTER IV

1. Yoder & Graves 2000; Donmoyer 2013.

2. Nutting, Wallace. 1924. *Pennsylvania Beautiful*. Framingham, MA: Old America Company Publishers.

3. Yoder & Graves 2000.

4. See "Hexerei & Ritual Harm" in Donmoyer, Patrick J. 2018. *Powwowing in Pennsylvania: Braucherei & the Ritual of Everyday Life*. Kutztown, PA: Pennsylvania German Cultural Heritage Center, Kutztown University of Pennsylvania, 175-195.

5. Ibid, 175.

6. According to former Windsor Township Supervisor Ernest Heckman, the township was asked to officially name the road in the 1970s, which had formerly been a significant artery between Virginville and Hamburg yet had no other name than the local name of "Hexebarrich" in the dialect. The township decided upon the name "Witchcraft Road" after careful consideration of the Pennsylvania Dutch name.

7. Donmoyer 2018.

8. This story was passed from Ellen E. (Hill) Heffner to her son Lee S. Heffner, and was discussed in interviews conducted in 2019-2020.

9. This same ritual is described annually at the Kutztown Folk Festival Seminar Stage by Leroy F. Brown (b. 1924) of Topton, Berks County in his presentation "Life of a Dutchman."

10. See "Powwow & The Authorities: Medical, Legal, Educational, Media" in Donmoyer 2018.

11. Donmoyer, Patrick J. 2014 "The Concealment of Blessings in Pennsylvania Barns." *Historical Archaeology: Manifestations of Magic: The Archaeology and Material Culture of Folk Religion*. Montclair, NJ: Society for Historical Archaeology, XL(6):179-195.

12. DeChant 1958: 55; Zehner 1953: 16.

13. Nutting 1924: 28.

14. "Hexefuss" in Henry Chapman Mercer Collection, Archaeological Research Notes. Folder 17. "Madrid, Delaware Valley, Yucatan Field notes. Including notes for Tamanend article, draft of Lehigh Hills papers for magazine, sunbonnets, Powwow formulae, Macungie notes" FH 150. 1863-1930. Bucks County Historical Society, Mercer Museum Archive.

15. Schlereth, Thomas J. 1999. *Material Culture Studies in America*. Walnut Creek, CA: AltaMira Press, 16-17.

16. Fogel 1995.

17. Long, Amos. 1972. *The Pennsylvania German Family Farm: A Regional Architectural and Folk Cultural Study of an American Agricultural Community*. Breinigsville, PA: Pennsylvania German Society. See also: "Myth of the Hex Sign" in Donmoyer 2013.

18. Yoder & Graves 2000.

19. A photograph appearing in the sports section of the *New York Daily News* on Friday, August 20,1948 shows Billy Southworth of the Atlanta Braves putting the "hex sign" on the Brooklyn Dodgers.

20. This appeared in a caption below Vincent R. Tortora's image of Milton Hill in his studio, in the *New York Times* on Sunday, June 17, 1962.

21. There are several examples of this in the Kutztown area, most notably, the restoration of the barn at the Isaac Bieber homestead of 1801. Others include the property of the "Burkholder's Produce" stand, which was restored by the owner, but later covered over with white metal siding, as well as the property of the Sauder's roadside market.

22. Foreword by Don Yoder, in Donmoyer 2013.

ENDNOTES

CHAPTER V

1. For the most recent history of the Kutztown Folk Festival, see: Donmoyer, Patrick J. 2019. "Kutztown Folk Festival: America's Oldest Folklife Celebration." *Pennsylvania Heritage.* Spring 2019. Harrisburg, PA: Pennsylvania Heritage Foundation.

2. Yoder, Don. 1963. "The Folklife Studies Movement." *Pennsylvania Folklife.* Summer XIII(3): 43-55.

3. Zehner introduces Milton Hill as a new artist at the Festival in the summer of 1953 in Zehner, Olive. 1953. "Folk Festival Dinkelfoodles." *Pennsylvania Dutchman.* V(4): 16.

4. Fooks, David. 2004. "The History of Pennsylvania's Barn Stars and Hex Signs" *Material Culture.* Fall XXXVI(20): 1-7. This account was repeated in Donmoyer 2013.

5. Interview with Esther (Hill) Derr, Harold Derr, and Lee S. Heffner, October 8, 2012.

6. Shoemaker, Alfred L., Don Yoder & J. William Frey. 1950. *The Pennsylvania Dutch Folk Festival Program.* Lancaster: Pennsylvania Dutch Folklore Center, Franklin and Marshall College.

7. Shoemaker, Alfred L. 1951. "Festival to Sponsor Tours Through the Dutch Country." III(5): 4.

8. Zehner 1953: 16.

9. Donmoyer 2019 & 2013. See also: "Hex of a Way to Make a Living." *Pittsburgh Press.* Sunday, Sept 25, 1955. The earliest known dated Ott hex sign is dated "June 1951" and is in the collection of Steve Stetzler of the Deitsch Eck Restaurant, formerly the Lenhartsville Hotel, in Lenhartsville, Berks County.

10. *New York Times* on Sunday, June 17, 1962.

11. Clippings from the *Reading Eagle*, show Arlene Francis surrounded by Milton's stars, while interviewing Festival director Dr. Alfred L. Shoemaker, and Milton J. Hill, who is incorrectly identified as "Martin Hill." The dates of these clippings in the collection of Lee S. Heffner are unknown, but likely July 3rd or 4th of 1954.

12. Shoemaker, Alfred L., Don Yoder & J. William Frey. 1961. *Program: The Pennsylvania Dutch Harvest Frolic.* Lancaster, PA: Pennsylvania Folklife Society. The grounds for the Folklife Society's museum were situated between Rt. 30 and Rockvale Road, bordered on one side by Hartman Bridge Road. This site today is the location of the Rockvale Outlets, and nothing is left of the brick barn and farmhouse.

13. A full photograph of the brick barn is included in the 1963 Summer issue of *Pennsylvania Folklife* XIII(3).

14. Tortora, Vincent R. 1966 & 1980. *Pennsylvania Dutch Hex Signs Illustrated in Natural Color: Their Origins, History, Usage, and Significance.* Manheim: Photo Arts Press.

15. Donmoyer 2019.

16. This passage is based on an interview with Milton Hill's granddaughter Dorian (Derr) Fetherolf.

17. Newspaper clipping "Church Rites Arranged for Accident Victim" *Reading Times.* Friday, July 12, 1963.

18. "Humphrey Visits Here to Press the Campaign of the Democratic Party." *Reading Eagle.* Thursday, October 15, 1964.

19. Vincent R. Tortora's photo essays and articles included: "The Amish at Play." *The Pennsylvania Dutchman.* Fall 1957.VIII(4):14; "The Courtship and Wedding Practices of the Old Order Amish." *The Pennsylvania Dutchman.* Spring 1958. IX(2):12; "The Get-Togethers of the Young Amish Folk." *The Pennsylvania Dutchman.* Spring 1960. XI(1):17; "The Amish in Their One-Room Schoolhouses." *The Pennsylvania Dutchman.* Summer 1960. XI(2):42; "Amish Barn Raisings." *The Pennsylvania Dutchman.* Fall 1961. XII(3):14;* etc.

20. Penny Wood of Ocean Grove, NJ, is identified in a newspaper clipping from the June 20, 1965. The clipping includes a special feature from "the staff of the Bulletin" - possibly clipped from the *Bergen News-Sun Bulletin* a newspaper in Palisades Park, New Jersey.

21. Bonner, Ruth E. 1965. *Sesqui-Centennial Commemorative Book, Kutztown, Pennsylvania 1815-1965.* Kutztown, PA: Kutztown Sesqui-Centennial Association, 114.

ENDNOTES

CHAPTER VI

1. An exchange with Milton about this was published in Tortora, Vincent. R. [ca. 1962.] *The Plain People.* Manheim, PA: Photo Arts Press, 57. Milton's stove was identified by Michael Emery of Cornwall Iron Furnace as a "Magnet Egg Stove," patented October 17, 1866 by Orr, Painter & Co. of the Reading Stove and Hollow-Ware Works, and featured in the 1873 *Catalogue and Price List of the Reading Stove & Hollow-Ware Works.* Reading, PA: Owen's Steam Book and Job Printing Office, 38-39.

2. Interview with Esther (Hill) Derr, Harold Derr, and Lee S. Heffner, October 8, 2012.

3. Deed Book 1593: 532. October 12, 1970. Office of the Berks County Recorder of Deeds.

4. A clipping, likely from the *Hamburg Item* outlines the festivities on the day of their anniversary.

5. Interview with Lee S. Heffner, December 2018.

6. Obituary, "Hill Rites Held in Perry Church," *Hamburg Item,* Jan 6, 1972.

7. Interviews with Lee S. Heffner, December 2019-2020.

8. Interviews with Dorian (Derr) Fetherolf, 2019-2020.

9. Obituary, Gertrude D. Hill, *Reading Eagle,* Oct 20, 1978.

CHAPTER VII

1. See: Historic American Buildings Survey, Historic American Engineering Record, Historic American Landscapes Survey, Library of Congress. <https://www.loc.gov/pictures/collection/hh/>

2. Shoemaker, Alfred L., Don Yoder & J. William Frey. 1950. *The Pennsylvania Dutch Folk Festival Program.* Lancaster: Pennsylvania Dutch Folklore Center, Franklin and Marshall College.

3. Hamburg Item Early Files, compiled by Peggy Sterner, July 16, 2020. See also: Fooks, David. 2004. "The History of Pennsylvania's Barn Stars and Hex Signs" *Material Culture.* Fall XXXVI(20): 1-7.

4 These differences can be seen in examples of Harry Adam's work featured in Smith, Elmer L. and Mel Horst. 1965. *Hex Signs and Other Barn Decorations.* Witmer, PA: Applied Arts.

5. "The Claypoole Legacy" in Donmoyer, 2013.

Milton J. Hill painting at the Kutztown Folk Festival ca. 1960. *Courtesy of Lee S. Heffner & Family.*

BIBLIOGRAPHY

--- ---. 1873. *Catalogue and Price List of the Reading Stove & Hollow-Ware Works*. Reading, PA: Owen's Steam Book and Job Printing Office.

Barr, Janet et al. 2007. *History of the Hamburg Area Volume II 1850-2000: 150 Years of Progress*. Kutztown, PA: Kutztown Publishing Co.

Beers, J. H. 1914. *Armstrong County, Pennsylvania: Her People, Past and Present*. Chicago: J. H. Beers & Co.

Bonner, Ruth E. 1965. *Sesqui-Centennial Commemorative Book, Kutztown, Pennsylvania 1815-1965*. Kutztown, PA: Kutztown Sesqui-Centennial Association.

Burgert, Annette Kunselman. 2000. *Palatine Origins of Some Pennsylvania Pioneers*. Myerstown, PA: AKB Publications.

DeChant, Alliene S. 1958. "Barn Sign Painter." *Historical Review of Berks County*. Spring XXIII(2): 54 55.

Donmoyer, Patrick J. 2019. "Kutztown Folk Festival: America's Oldest Folklife Celebration." *Pennsylvania Heritage*. Spring 2019. Harrisburg, PA: Pennsylvania Heritage Foundation.

Donmoyer, Patrick J. 2019. *Hex Signs: Sacred and Celestial Symbolism in Pennsylvania Dutch Barn Stars*. A Collaborative Exhibition at Glencairn Museum. Kutztown, PA: Pennsylvania German Cultural Heritage Center, Kutztown University.

Donmoyer, Patrick J. 2018. *Powwowing in Pennsylvania: Braucherei & the Ritual of Everyday Life*. Kutztown, PA: Pennsylvania German Cultural Heritage Center, Kutztown University of Pennsylvania.

Donmoyer, Patrick J. 2014 "The Concealment of Blessings in Pennsylvania Barns," *Historical Archaeology: Manifestations of Magic: The Archaeology and Material Culture of Folk Religion*. Montclair, NJ: Society for Historical Archaeology, XL(6):179-195.

Donmoyer, Patrick J. 2013. *Hex Signs: Myth and Meaning in Pennsylvania Dutch Barn Stars*. Kutztown, PA: Pennsylvania German Cultural Heritage Center, Kutztown University.

Fogel, Edwin Miller. 1995. *Beliefs and Superstitions of the Pennsylvania Germans*.

Fooks, David. 2004. "The History of Pennsylvania's Barn Stars and Hex Signs" *Material Culture*. Fall XXXVI(20): 1-7.

Fooks, David. 2003. "The History of Hex Signs." The Pennsylvania German Review, Fall 2003. Kutztown, PA: Pennsylvania German Cultural Heritage Center.

Fooks, David. 2002. "In Search of America's Oldest Hex Signs," Der Reggeboge 36(1):21–27

Kidd, H.S. 1923. *Lutherans in Berks County; Two Centuries of Continuous Organized Church Life 1723-1923*. Reading, PA: Reading Conference of the Evangelical Lutheran Ministerium of Pennsylvania

Long, Amos, Jr. 1972. *The Pennsylvania German Family Farm: A Regional Architectural and Folk Cultural Study of an American Agricultural Community*. Breinigsville, PA: Pennsylvania German Society.

Meiser, George M. IX. 1998. *The Passing Scene XI*. Reading, PA: Reading Eagle Press.

Nutting, Wallace. 1924. *Pennsylvania Beautiful*. Framingham, MA: Old America Company Publishers.

Shoemaker, Alfred L. 1955. *The Pennsylvania Barn*. Lancaster: Pennsylvania Dutch Folklore Center, Inc., Franklin and Marshall College.

Shoemaker, Alfred L. *Hex No!* 1953. Lancaster: Pennsylvania Dutch Folklore Center, Franklin and Marshall College.

Shoemaker, Alfred L., Don Yoder & J. William Frey. 1950. *The Pennsylvania Dutch Folk Festival Program*. Lancaster: Pennsylvania Dutch Folklore Center, Franklin and Marshall College.

Shoemaker, Alfred L., Don Yoder & J. William Frey. 1961. *Program: The Pennsylvania Dutch Harvest Frolic*. Lancaster, PA: Pennsylvania Folklife Society.

Smith, Elmer L. and Mel Horst. 1965. *Hex Signs and Other Barn Decorations*. Witmer, PA: Applied Arts.

Strassburger, Ralph Beaver & John William Hinke. 1992. *Pennsylvania German Pioneers*. Camden, ME: Picton Press, Vol I.

Stoever, John Casper. 1984. *Early Lutheran Baptisms and Marriages in Southeastern Pennsylvania: The Records of John Casper Stoever from 1730-1779*. Baltimore: Genealogical Publishing Company.

Tortora, Vincent R. 1966 & 1980. *Pennsylvania Dutch Hex Signs Illustrated in Natural Color: Their Origins, History, Usage, and Significance*. Manheim: Photo Arts Press.

Tortora, Vincent. R. 1962. *The Plain People*. Manheim, PA: Photo Arts Press, 57.

Trexler, Mark K. 1959. *The Lutheran Church in Berks County*. Kutztown, PA: Kutztown Publishing Company.

Yoder, Don. 2015. *Discovering American Folklife*. Kutztown, PA: Pennsylvania German Cultural Heritage Center, Kutztown University.

Yoder, Don & Thomas E. Graves. 2000. *Hex Signs: Pennsylvania Dutch Barn Symbols and Their Meanings*. 2nd Ed. Mechanicsburg, PA: Stackpole Books

Yoder, Don. 1963. "The Folklife Studies Movement." *Pennsylvania Folklife*. Summer XIII(3): 43-55.

Zehner, Olive. 1953. "The Hills from Hamburg." *Pennsylvania Dutchman*. IV(11): 16, 13. Lancaster, PA: Pennsylvania Dutch Folklore Center, Franklin & Marshall College.

A weathered "Ghost Project" by Eric Claypoole of Lenhartsville, featuring an elaborate Milton Hill Star, painted on bare wood in order to observe the differential weathering process of the sun's rays. *Courtesy of Eric Claypoole.*

INDEX

Abraham Lincoln Hotel, Reading City   90-91
Adam, Elmer D.   36
Adam, Harry L.   96-98, 108, 110
Adam, Jeremiah P. (1880-1966)   24, 32, 133
Adam, Oscar   34-35 116,
Adam, Wilson   34-35
Allentown Band   18
Allentown, Lehigh County   18, 36, 88, 95, 134
Amish communities   66, 67, 79, 86, 87, 136
asafetida   63
Balthaser, Myers, Car Dealership   18
bank barn (see also Pennsylvania Barn)   14, 46, 55, 58-59
barn blessing   64-65
barn star   15, 32
Berks County   13, 20, 21, 15, 29, 30, 33, 35, 39, 40, 61-63, 65, 67, 70, 85, 88, 101
Berstler, Milton   36
Bethlehem, Northampton County   19, 27
Billig, Allen J.   92
Blessing, Joanna   95, 112-113
Blumme (flowers)   32, 134
Braucherei (*Brauche*, powwowing)   63-65
Buick Special   18, 80
Burgert, Annette K.   133
Burkey & Spacht Funeral Home, Hamburg   92-93
Chupy (Hill Family dog)   48
Claypoole, Eric A.   32, 95-96, 98, 100-101, 104-107, 108, 111, 112-113, 115-117, 120, 123, 127-129, 132
Claypoole, John (Johnny) P.   98, 104-105, 114-115
Davis, Gwenny   71
Deischer, Henry K.   95, 102
Derr, Esther L. (Hill)   6-7. 15, 17-18, 20, 24-25, 34-35, 37-38, 41, 43, 46, 49, 53-55, 57, 77, 80, 90-93, 134
Derr, Harold J.   6, 7, 20, 24-25, 35, 37, 38, 41, 46, 48, 54, 77, 80, 84, 91, 92, 93, 135, 137

Die Hoiet (first hay cutting)   57
Die Ohmet (second hay cutting)   57
Dietrich, Wallace. A.   34, 35, 95, 134
Dietrich's Meats & Country Store   126
District Township, Berks County   114
Donmoyer, Patrick J.   6, 7, 19, 94, 95, 96, 98, 100, 101, 103, 105, 107, 109-117, 119, 128-129, 130
Dornbusch, Charles H.   95, 99
Dreibelbis, John   36
Dreibelbis, William   18
Dreibelbis Station Covered Bridge   127
Dries, Maurice J.   25, 27
"Dumb Dutch" stereotype   66
Earl Township, Berks County   62-63, 114
Edris, Sarah E.   80, 129-131
Farmall Tractor   16-17, 56,
Ferrell, William E.   95, 97, 99-101
Fetherolf, Dorian L. (Derr)   6, 7, 46, 53-54, 57, 75, 77, 80, 84, 91, 93, 135-137
Fleetwood, Berks County   39
Folklife   29, 43, 60, 64, 66-67, 69-70, 76, 78-79, 81, 83, 86, 87, 136
Fooks, David   97, 107, 134, 136
Framingham, Massachusetts   61
Francis, Arlene   75
Frey, Dr. J. William   16, 67, 69
Fritch, Dr. Milton   18
Fry, Mabel M. (Heffner)   53, 75, 69,
Fry, Phares W.   69, 75, 92
Fry, Valerie E.   53
ghost (solar weathering)   40-41, 105, 109, 120, 132
Graver, Jason   72-73
Greenwich Township, Berks County   110, 112, 116
Gruber's School House, Perry Township   53
Guldin, Charles   36
Hamburg, Berks County   13, 19, 39, 71, 77, 82, 83, 92, 107, 109, 124, 133-135, 137

141

Harry Dreibelbis   18

Harvest Frolic, Lancaster   66, 71, 79, 87

Heckman, Curtin   36

Heffner, Betty J.   53-54

Heffner, Ellen E. (Hill)   48, 53-55, 64, 93, 133

Heffner, Lee S.   6, 7, 9, 15-19, 23, 25, 27, 38-39, 47, 48, 50-51, 54-57, 68, 70, 74, 82-83, 90, 92, 133, 135, 136, 137

Heffner, Stanley O.   15, 36, 39, 54,

Hepner, Samuel   30, 32, 134

Herring, Timothy   122

Hertzog, Phares H.   111

Heuchelheim, Frankenthal, Germany   21, 133

hex signs   13, 15, 32, 41, 60- 67, 98, 134

Hex Tour Association   97, 107, 117,

Hexebarrich (Witchcraft Hill)   63-65

Hexologist   75

Heyl, John K.   95

Hill & Strausser   54

Hill Barn   25, 42, 43, 46, 48, 50-51, 54-59, 82

Hill Family   15-27, 29-30, 33-34, 39, 42-59, 80-82, 84, 90-93

Hill Farm, Perry Township, Berks County   15-19, 21-27, 42-59, 81-84, 91-93

Hill Star   12-16, 24, 28-32, 41, 68-71, 74, 75, 80, 81, 83-85, 91, 93, 96-110, 114-116, 118, 120-133

Hill, Agnes A. I. (Brobst)   53-54, 93

Hill, Anna E.   54

Hill, Anna Elisabetha (Müller) (1691-1774)   21

Hill, Catherine S. "Cass" (Berstler)   25, 36

Hill, Daniel T.   54, 92

Hill, Ellen E. (Wanner)   20, 23, 27, 63-64, 81

Hill, Gertrude D. (Strausser)   15-19, 27, 42-58, 90-93

Hill, Jacob W.   15, 39, 43, 53-54,

Hill, Jacob, Jr. (b. 1818)   21

Hill, Jacob, Sr. (1789-1885)   23, 25

Hill, Johann Jacob (1689-1739)   21

Hill, Johann Jacob (1716-1775)   21-23

Hill, John L.   15, 39, 41, 43, 50, 53-54, 80-82, 96-97

Hill, John M.   22-25, 29-30, 33-34, 43-46

Hill, John T.   23-25, 27, 36

Hill, June R. (Schappell)   54, 80

Hill, Magdalena (Strausser)   23, 25

Hill, Maria Apollonia (Merkel) (1719-1774)   21

Hill, Mary (Miller) (1822-1880)   23

Hill, Mary G.   54

Hill, Melva V. (Brobst)   53-54

Hill, Patricia I.   54

Hill, Robert M.   54, 80, 92

Hill, William T.   54, 92

Hinnershitz, Mabel (Strausser)   49

Hoch, George K.   36, 37, 134

Hoffa, Paul   36-37

Hoffa, Sallie D. (Strausser)   36, 49, 76, 92

Homan, Chester & Esther   18

"Home" on NBC   75

Hoyt, Ivan E.   12-14, 19, 121, 125

Humma, Beth A. (Hill)   6, 23, 26, 42, 49, 82,

Humphrey, Hubert H.   84-85

Keener, Rev. Thomas J.   92

Keim, George   36

Kempton, Berks County   19, 39

Kistler Snyder Barn   95, 112-113

Kohler Ice Cream Plant   32

Kutztown Day   19

Kutztown Folk Festival   13-19, 33, 41, 67-89, 91, 96, 97, 102, 107, 117, 121, 130-131, 134-136

Kutztown Sesqui-Centennial Celebration   88-89

Kutztown State College (See also Kutztown University)   19, 88-89

Kutztown University   7, 15, 19, 20, 24, 25, 33, 35, 37, 40, 41, 66, 67, 70, 77, 80, 81, 85, 87-89, 97, 99, 100, 102, 117, 130-131

Kutztown, Berks County   13-19, 41, 67-89, 91, 131-132

Lambsheim, Frankenthal, Germany   21

Langkamer, Rev. Lynn L.   93

Lauer's Brewery, Reading   15

Lebanon County   67

Lehigh County   32, 61, 63, 65, 67, 95, 96, 114

Leiby Farm, Windsor Township   33, 60, 103

Lenhartsville, Berks County   32, 39, 60, 71, 75, 95, 96, 98, 100, 105, 107, 109, 111-112, 114, 128, 132, 136
Lonergan, Melvin S.   111
Lower Macungie, Lehigh County   114
Lukens, Ernest & Dorothy (Mull)   93
McCormick-Deering Tractor   17, 56, 57,
Meisenheim, Frankenthal, Germany   21, 134
Mennonite communities   66-67
Merkel Family   21
Miller, Viola   18
Moselem Springs, Berks County   21, 23, 35, 36
mouse trap   26, 27
Moyer, Russell   18
Moyer, Walter   36
Mull, Chester   93
Muller, Carol S. (Hill)   54, 80
Murray, Jack   107
Myers, Dr. Albertus L.   18
Nutting, Wallace   61-65
Ocean Grove, New Jersey   88-89
Oley Valley, Berks County   115
Onyx Cave, Perry Township   103
Ott, John J. "Johnny"   75
Penn Square, Reading City   85
Pennsylvania Barn (see also bank barn)   14, 29, 33, 42-46, 48, 55, 58-59 62, 95
Pennsylvania Dutch Folklore Center, Franklin & Marshall College, Lancaster (See Pennsylvania Folklife Society)
Pennsylvania Dutch Language   23, 32, 50, 57, 63-65, 83
Pennsylvania Dutchman   16, 34, 62, 64, 87
Pennsylvania Folklife   87
Pennsylvania Folklife Society   16, 28-29, 60, 66-67, 69-71, 76, 78-79, 81. 86-87
Pennsylvania German Cultural Heritage Center, Kutztown University   14, 46, 55, 58-59
Pennsylvania Triennial Farm Census   43, 46
Perry Township, Berks County   19-21, 23, 31, 43, 53, 98, 103, 133
Philadelphia, Pennsylvania   21
Plain Communities   66-67

Powwowing (*Braucherei, Brauch*e)   63-65
Rausch, Allen   30-32
Rausch, Thomas   32
Reading Stoveworks, Orr, Painter & Co.   91
Reidel, Billy   100-101
Reinert, Guy F.   95
remedies   51, 53, 64
Richmond Township, Berks County   36, 117
Ruscombmanor Township, Berks County   108
Schappell Family   23, 36, 47, 54, 80
Schappell, Albert M.   47
Schappell, Eva M.   47
Schappell, George   36
Schappell, James M.   47
Schappell, Margaret S. (Mengel)   47
Schappell, Sassaman J.   47
Schtanne (stars)   32, 134
Shartlesville, Berks County   102, 109
Shire Valley Legacies   23, 26, 42, 49, 82
Shirk, Andrew   107, 124, 125, 122, 128-129
Shoemaker, Dr. Alfred L.   14, 16, 41, 64, 67, 69-71, 74-75, 79, 96, 134, 136
Shoemakersville, Berks County   19, 27, 43, 54
Shults, Rev. Peter S.   93
Smith, Daniel L.   32
Smith, Donald I.   29, 32
Smith, Ethel   82-83
Stein Farm, Virginville   24, 35
Stichter's Hardware Store, Reading   15
Strausser, Hettie Y. (Dreibelbis)   27, 47
Strausser, John Reuben   27, 47
Strausser, Ollie   18
Strausser, Warren D   54
Stump, Anson   18
Sunday Farm, Perry Township   98, 104-105,
Tortora, Vincent R.   79, 83, 85-89
tourism   32, 61-62, 64-67
Virginville Community Grange #1832   126
Virginville, Berks County   13, 15, 18-19, 21, 24, 29, 33-35, 37, 39, 46, 51, 54-55, 60, 80, 82, 84, 94, 96-98, 105, 107, 112, 116, 128, 133, 135, 141
Wagenhurst, Charles   18

wallpaper   38

Wash, Katherine M.   131

Weiss, Rev. Benjamin   20

Windsor Castle, Berks County   23, 27, 29, 30, 32, 39-41, 92, 93

Windsor Dairy   32

Windsor Township, Berks County   21, 23, 35, 63, 93

Witchcraft Road, Windsor Township   63-64

Wood, Penny   88-89

Works Progress Administration (WPA)   48

Yoder, Dr. Don   16, 33, 67, 69, 135-136

Yoder, Robert   36

Zechman, Rev. Herbert B.   92

Zehner, Olive G.   16, 41, 69, 71

Zion (Reformed) United Church of Christ, Windsor Castle   23, 93

Zion Lutheran Church, Windsor Castle   23

Zion Moselem Lutheran Church   21, 23

Zion Union Cemetery   93

Zion Union Church, Windsor Castle   20, 23, 27